THE TWELVE HEALERS OF THE ZODIAC

Peter Damian

THE
TWELVE
HEALERS
OF THE
ZODIAC

The Astrology
Handbook of the
Bach Flower
Remedies

SAMUEL WEISER, INC.
York Beach, Maine

First published in 1986 by
Samuel Weiser, Inc.
Box 612
York Beach, Maine 03910

Second printing, 1991

Library of Congress Cataloging - in - Publication Data

Damian, Peter.
    The twelve healers of the zodiac.

    Bibliography: p.
    Includes index.
    1. Astrology and health.   2. Healing - - Miscelanea.
I.   Title.
BF1729.H9D36   1986   133.5'861   86-1652

ISBN 0-87728-653-1
MG

Typeset in 10 pt. Souvenir
Printed in the United States of America

CONTENTS

For Kit

An Astrologer's Prayer

Heavenly Parent, both Father and Mother,
assist me in my assistance to others.

PREFACE

This book is both an astrological study and a practical handbook for the Bach Flower Remedies.* It contains descriptions of the original remedies known as the Twelve Healers, and establishes the astrological correspondences, while providing a simple and accurate astrological method for their use.

With this handbook, I seek to demonstrate the usefulness of astrology when its symbolism is applied to a better understanding of any circumstance or system. The astrological correlations also serve to prompt and perpetuate the work of Dr. Edward Bach, who discovered the therapy of flower remedies. For astrology students and practitioners to whom the Bach Remedies are still unfamiliar, the handbook will introduce a new and exciting astrological system of study. By combining these two bodies of knowledge in practical application, we can improve upon ourselves, improve upon our astrological skills, and acquire one more means by which we may be of great benefit and assistance to others.

For those adherents of Dr. Bach's work who are unacquainted with astrology, this handbook can serve as an introduction. It will, at the very least, be a source of worthwhile information concerning the remedies themselves.

The traits of the twelve astrological signs are virtually identical with those ascribed by Bach to the Twelve Healers. As you read the

---

*Bach, as he is known in England, is pronounced "batch."

personality traits of the flower-type described in Bach's sequential order, you will see the traits of the Sun signs. For example, the Agrimony type described by Bach relates to the Sagittarian type described by astrologers. If we wish to overcome some of the less attractive traits of the sign types, the Bach Remedies may provide the necessary emotional changes necessary so that we can accomplish this, either on a personal level, or for our clients.

In this writer's opinion, an astrological appreciation of the marvelous work done by Edward Bach with his flowers only confirms its grand significance. I have faith in astrology. I have faith in the Bach Flower Remedies. I would like to believe that Edward Bach's blessings accompany my effort to unite the two within these pages.

Peter Damian

CHAPTER 1

THE TWELVE HEALERS

The Bach Flower Remedies are a simple and natural method of healing (or establishing equilibrium and harmony) through the personality using the essences of wild flowers. The pharmacopoeia for this method of treatment is made up of thirty-eight flower remedies. Bach therapy was discovered and developed in England by Edward Bach, a scientist, bacteriologist, and physician who made his discoveries in the 1920s and 1930s. He made his remedies from wild plants, bushes, or trees, and they were directed at relieving mental states. They were not prescribed for physical complaints, but were used according to the patient's state of mind. The theory was based upon the understanding that an inharmonious state of mind accompanies all diseases, and a negative mental condition may, in fact, be the primary cause for the sickness. Left untreated the mental state will continue to hinder the recovery. The Bach Flower Remedies are still decidedly holistic in their applica-tion—they treat the patient and not the disease.

The remedies are simple, safe, and inexpensive. Readily avail-able without written prescription, none are harmful or habit-forming. They bear no antagonism to any other form of medical treatment, and can be safely used by anyone. It was Edward Bach's intention that any person could bring about self-healing by means of these flower essences. A few drops in water or under the tongue, taken from a prepared bottle, is all that is necessary.

The most important application of the remedies is their use as a preventative measure, encouraging people to become attuned to their own mental and spiritual condition or well-being, and to seek and apply remedy to any discord that exists at causal levels of being. By treating causal levels first, the remedies allow us to dispel this disharmony at its source, prior to its manifestation as physical disease. Bach had this to say concerning this matter:

> The action of these remedies is to raise our vibrations and open up our channels for the reception of the Spiritual Self; to flood our natures with the particular virtue we need, and wash out from us the fault which is causing the harm. They are able, like beautiful music or any glorious or uplifting thing which gives us inspiration, to raise our very natures, and bring us nearer to our souls and by that very act to bring us peace and relieve our sufferings. They cure, not by attacking the disease, but by flooding our bodies with the beautiful vibrations of our Higher Nature, in the presence of which, disease melts away as snow in the sunshine.
>
> There is no true healing unless there is a change in outlook, peace of mind, and inner happiness.[1]

I don't feel that Bach ever meant the flower remedies to be therapeutic in the exact sense of curing a particular disease. We can use them to assist and inspire the mind and spirit. Disease cannot thrive where a state of health exists. True health is more than the absence of illness or pain, it is a radiant condition of vibrancy. The outflowing power of health, like the rays of the sun, does not allow the entrance of darkness or disease. The flower remedies uplift both spirit and mind, raising the level of Life Energy within us, helping us create a condition of true health.

There are thirty-eight Remedies in the Bach system of healing. Originally there were only twelve. Bach discovered the twelve healers between 1928 and 1932. The twelve healers are described in

---

[1]Philip M. Chancellor: *Handbook of the Bach Flower Remedies*, C. W. Daniel Co., Ltd., Saffron Walden, England, 1971, and Keats Publishing, New Canaan, CT. From the Proem by Bach, p. 13.

a pamphlet published shortly after his discovery.[2] Bach's work with flowers was prompted by his realization that the whole of humanity was composed of twelve definite, grouped types. Every individual belongs to one of these groupings, sharing in common distinct traits of character, personality, and temperament. The members of each group are, according to Bach, clearly recognizable by behavior, attitude, and expression. The various types became especially evident in times of illness, Bach observed.

Rather than treating disease, Bach treated his patient's personality, character, and mood. Inspired by his observations, Bach concentrated on researching the moods from which the twelve differing types suffer, and discovered that there were twelve outstanding states of mind:

1. Fear
2. Terror
3. Mental torture or worry
4. Indecision
5. Indifference or boredom
6. Doubt or discouragement
7. Over-concern
8. Weakness
9. Self-distrust
10. Impatience
11. Over-enthusiasm
12. Pride or aloofness[3]

These twelve states of mind correspond to the twelve healers that Bach sought as remedies. The twelve signs of the zodiac correspond to the twelve healers as each sign type has a weakness that can be overcome as we evolve.

It is interesting to note that Bach relied on his intuition in the process of discovering and preparing his flower essences. He did not conduct "scientific" experiments. He was attuned to the

---

[2]Edward Bach: *The Twelve Healers and Other Remedies,* C. W. Daniel Co., Ltd., Saffron Walden, England. Also available under the title *The Bach Remedies,* published by Keats Publishing, New Canaan, CT.

[3]Nora Weeks: *The Medical Discoveries of Edward Bach Physician,* C. W. Daniel Co., Ltd., Saffron Walden, England, and Keats Publishing, New Canaan, CT. p. 62.

archetypal order that dictates natural laws and does govern natural processes. I assess that his division of humanity into twelve types was neither an arbitrary nor a coincidental classification in the colloquial sense.[4] Rather, it was coincidental in the archetypal understanding of the word, highlighting to the occult or astrologically-minded reader the significant emergence of the numbers twelve and seven in all of Edward Bach's classifications. To say that Bach was partial to these archetypal-numerical systems is clearly evident in his work: the twelve types of humanity, the twelve flower remedies or healers, twelve outstanding states of mind. Also note the seven headings under which Bach later grouped all thirty-eight essences. In his book *Heal Thyself*, Bach listed what he believed to be the real and primary diseases of man: pride, cruelty, hate, self-love, ignorance, instability, and greed.[5] Once again, seven in number. Even prior to his exclusive devotion to the flower work, when he was still in practice as a bacteriologist, Bach became known for his Bach Nosodes. These *seven* nosodes (vaccines)— which are still in use today—are administered orally to combat the enormous variety of organisms present in the intestine. These varieties were classified by Bach, and he named the *seven* groups of bacilli that constitute the seven main groups!

I truly believe these numerical values—twelve and seven—to be sacred to Nature; and that they occurred as natural order to Edward Bach, to both house and illustrate his personal archetypal inspirations and discoveries.[6]

Still, the corresponding proof of the twelve healers to the twelve signs of the zodiac is not left solely to the numbers. Following are comprehensive descriptions of the twelve flower-types of personality and the moods for which they are prescribed. To each I have attached the corresponding astrological sign. It will

---

[4]The signficance has not in any way been diluted by the fact that Bach later added twenty-six additional remedies, as we will discuss later.

[5]Edward Bach: *Heal Thyself*, C. W. Daniel Co., Ltd., Saffron Walden, England. Also available under the title *The Bach Remedies*, published by Keats Publishing, New Canaan, CT. p. 15.

[6]None of the related intimations concerning Bach's numerical or archetypal intuitions will surprise the reader who understands that Bach was a Mason.

be easy for the astrologer to appreciate how each depiction of remedy-type in turn offers a unique and fascinating profile of its corresponding zodiacal sign.

AGRIMONY
(Agrimonia eupatoria)

People who require Agrimony convey a good-spirited manner which disguises minds in turmoil. On the surface they appear carefree. This is only a cheerful facade, disguising inner worries which are seldom discussed. Agrimony types are peace-loving and non-argumentative. Owning a delightful sense of humor, they make for good company. In truth, Agrimony types strongly desire and seek companionship as one means of escaping and forgetting their woes. While highly independent, they dislike being alone.

Their sense of humor is often put to the purpose of making light of personal discomforts and cares—especially regarding personal illness. In reality, however, these individuals are nervous and filled with anxiety concerning the future, fearing the prospect of contracting an illness that could curb activity. They fear restriction and love excitement and adventure. They are prone to experiencing periods of great restlessness. They may even resort to alcohol, drugs, gambling, or other excessive behavior, in order to dull or distract themselves from some inner worry.

The constructive Agrimony type is the true optimist. Bold, cheerful, and genial, they possess an ability to smile at misfortune. They securely laugh at their own cares, because they know what endures in life. These are people who are natural peacemakers—gladdening the hearts of all they meet. With natural enthusiasm, constructive Agrimony types are expansive and freedom-loving. They know how to bring others "out of themselves," improving their outlook upon life. "Hail fellow, well met!" is the maxim for Agrimony.

Sagittarius
Mutable—Fire
November 21–December 21

A study of this sign will offer valuable insight into the Agrimony type. Symbolized by the Centaur (upper half man/lower half horse), Sagittarius is the ninth sign of the zodiac. Because Sagittarius is a mutable fire sign, it combines qualities that account for a wayward (yet adaptable), enthusiastic (yet unbridled) temperament for those born under its influence. Put another way, as readily as the Centaur's mutable flame of inspiration is kindled, it just as easily goes out. This fact may not be obvious to the casual observer because the Sagittarian is ever camouflaging with humor and bravado. The Sagittarian types need encouragement more often than they are willing to let on. The flower remedy Agrimony supplies such encouragement in the most natural way.

Sagittarians are usually friendly, extroverted, and seemingly optimistic throughout any circumstance. They are sporting types, after all, and are very independent, acting more upon their own instincts than upon advice. Aspiring in their outlook upon life, they crave a variety of experience. In youth they are apt to procrastinate a great deal. They can be tactless and irresponsible but are not deliberately cruel. Unless we are discussing a Sagittarian under very negative aspects,[7] we can anticipate that experience will foster maturity eventually, and an inherent love of philosophy will manifest itself. The evolved Sagittarian harbors deep religious feeling within and often becomes intensely involved with matters ecclesiastical. Suddenly, the rebellious youth grows to become a pillar of the community. This is depicted by the dichotomous image of the Centaur—illustrating the eventual triumph of the human aspirations over the animal nature. Sagittarius is also the Archer and his arrow points the way of the "straight and narrow" path for the initiate seeking a higher consciousness. The Path of the Arrow is essentially a Qabalistic reference, and it is significant that Sagit-

---

[7]A natal chart said to be under very negative aspects would be one in which uncomplementary aspects between planets (squares, oppositions and certain conjunctions) are seen to predominate. These aspects produce friction, and, subsequently, non-constructive patterns of energy and behavior.

tarius is only the ninth sign, and the arrow it holds has yet to be released. It remains aimed, pointing straight upward and ahead to the last three signs, for they mirror the Supernal Triangle upon the Tree of Life, the highest aspect of god-consciousness. Chiron (a centaur) was a great teacher according to mythology; and the Sagittarian loves to preach and instruct whether the topic be religion or race horses. A fictional character who typifies this Sagittarian need to have his opinions respected above all else is Professor Henry Higgins in Shaw's *Pygmalion*, made famous by the musical, *My Fair Lady*. Another fictional Sagittarian would be "old Fezziwig" of Dickens' *A Christmas Carol*. His authentic generosity was boundless, persisting in the face of economic hardship.

CENTAURY
(Centaurium umbellatum)

People requiring Centaury are prone to a weakness of will which causes them to be too easily exploited or imposed upon—even to the point of servitude. Lacking individuality, Centaury types are shy and timid, and because they are overly anxious to please, they are easily dominated and manipulated. They may become docile, even submissive. They can easily be used by others, for they have difficulty saying "no," and are often overworked because of a willingness to serve. Easily exhausted physically, they are, nonetheless, mentally alert and active.

Centaury types have difficulty standing up for themselves. They are easily influenced. Advice from others only manages to further undermine and distort what little individuality they possess. For these people, life can be a drudgery of mundane tasks and details. They lack imagination. They may miss out on the joy in life by adhering too much to duties. (These duties may take the form of servitude to family or parents.) They may care for an unsympathetic boss or work for an unsympathetic master. Often they forego personal aspirations and wishes, in order to care for another. Thus they tend toward self-denial, or to self-martyrdom, which may take the form of stoically endured illness (or even hypochondria). Fond of convention, they are prone to let the tail wag the dog when it comes to conducting their lives. Just as fond of etiquette, they dislike contention and wouldn't think of making a scene.

The constructive Centaury type knows how—and whom—to serve. They do so calmly, quietly, efficiently, and with discretion. They are discriminating in their efforts on behalf of others and in their personal involvements. They participate in—but never succumb to—the collective, respecting more their own individuality and mission in life. For this they are respected for wise counsel and sincere dependability.

Virgo
Mutable—Earth
August 21–September 21

A study of this sign will offer valuable insight into the Centaury type. Virgo is the sixth sign of the zodiac. The image of the sign is the Virgin, which lends itself to the modest and dignified nature of those born under this sign. The Virgo does tend to the virtuous in conduct, sometimes to the point of repressiveness. This is a religious sign that expresses its nature in a need to serve. A Virgo can be an excellent nurse because the profession allows one to enjoy being helpful and efficient. Possessing a strong sense of detail, and acute powers of discrimination, Virgo is meticulous and has a practical nature. George Bernard Shaw's words, "The love of economy is the root of all virtue," could be made a motto for this sign. Virgo is certainly materialistic and exacting. Just as the physical body digests and assimilates, so does the Virgo mind.

The desire to be "appropriate" makes the Virgo overly conventional. Most secure in routine, often missing the magic in life (but yearning for it), Virgo may never realize that magic has no routine. The Virgo view of life can remain "microscopic" while the Sagittarian's is "telescopic." The Virgo is earnest and reliable. Astrological symbols describe the sign accurately—the time of Virgo is the time for harvest. Virgo symbolizes the bread, which, along with the fishes of its opposite sign Pisces, is all that is necessary to feed the multitude. The symbol of the caduceus is the expression of Virgo's ruling planet (Mercury) when it manifests in this sign. It is recognizable as the healing symbol of the physician, the rod of Asklepios. Virgo is "good bread" as the "staff of life" (caduceus) and those born to this sign are the pure and faithful.

CERATO
(Ceratostigma willmottiana)

Those who require Cerato lack confidence in self, and in personal judgment. As a result, and out of a genuine thirst for information on any subject, they constantly seek advice from others. No opinion is untrustworthy enough to be ignored, and they are therefore often misguided individuals! Ironically, Cerato types are knowledgeable, having a keen intelligence and definite opinions. They simply doubt their own choices and abilities. Following the advice of others, they are capable of the most foolish and gullible acts—always against their better judgment. They'll try anything upon advice or recommendation. This is due as much to natural inquisitiveness and a need for diversification, as it is to a lack of confidence.

Changeable, talkative, lacking in concentration, Cerato types manage to exhaust everyone around them with an endless stream of questions, seeking advice. They are thought to lack conviction because of this facet of personality. And often they do. It is their fear of being pinned down which is responsible for the nervous vacillation. At best, they lack continuity in thought and action.

Cerato types admire anyone who appears to know his own mind (or who knows about the Cerato type's mind!). They are attracted to people who demonstrate will-power and self-command, such as the Vervain or Water Violet types. The Cerato types admire people who can be optimistically confident (Agrimony type) or self-motivated (Impatiens type)—so much so that they will imitate them. The ability for mime can be confusing to others, for this type tends to exhibit the behavioral traits of the last person with whom they were in contact.

Similar to the Centaury type, the Cerato personality is fond of convention; for like Centaury, a need to have socially "correct" views is important. Convention gives the Cerato type confidence that "the right thing" is being done. He is on the "right" side, is making the "right" decision. Convention provides identity or purpose, serving as a defense against the fear of the unknown. The Cerato type differs from the weak-willed, easily persuaded Centaury type, in that Cerato knows who he or she is, and individuality grants the right to dismiss, rebel against, or otherwise flaunt these conventions on occasion—something the Centaury type would not consider. Contrastingly, too, the Cerato type is more attracted to novelty, and is less concerned with being of service to others.

The constructive Cerato type displays serene confidence. Like the owl, these people stand with a dignity and wisdom beyond their years. Very intuitive, Cerato types seek advice both from within and above, not relying only on other people. They are capable of making accurate judgments, trusting their own minds and abilities. They are comprehensive and capable, and usually function well no matter what the circumstances.

Gemini
Mutable—Air
May 21–June 21

A study of this sign will offer valuable insight into the Cerato type. Gemini is the third sign of the zodiac. The combination of the air element and mutable nature causes this sign to be the sign of motion and phenomena. Air symbolizes intelligence and lends a studious nature to the Gemini. The key words for this sign are, "I think." Geminis are always thinking. Like Virgo, Gemini is ruled by the planet Mercury, and the sign is imbued with Mercury's celestial brilliance, but in a different manner from that of Virgo. The caduceus symbol of Mercury for Gemini more appropriately represents Aaron's rod—Aaron of the *Old Testament* who was the voice for his brother Moses, interceding in matters of great importance to Israel, so great was his eloquence. Geminis are indeed well-spoken, more tactful than Sagittarians, and although they are less consistent and reliable than Virgoans, they are also less opinionated. Spontaneous, amusing, largely unpredictable, and in youth especially mischievous, their lack of discipline is a result of their many interests. They don't want to miss out on anything. They suffer from the kind of chronic awareness that is most noticeable in the Cerato type.

In China, Gemini is known as the monkey sign because of its restless, inquisitive, and imitative nature. We know it in the West as the Twins. The symbol for the sign bespeaks a certain duality. Often of two minds, sometimes cunningly two-faced, Geminis also have an uncanny knack for doing two things, or being in two places at one time. Perhaps it only appears that way, for these people can possess magnificent minds (twice the average brain power?) which place them among the giants in all fields. Highly sociable, the Twins also symbolize the Geminian need for companionship. They are not as freedom-loving as some might believe, and when you look closely you will realize Geminis are not really loners.

CHICORY
(Chicorium intybus)

People who require Chicory are blocking the impulse to stream forth unconditional love. When this energy is drawn inward, the normally outpouring forces of love, energy, and knowledge become dangerous and may be expressed, instead, as a concentric egoistic concern for power, or in a grasping covetousness.

Chicory types are jealous and possessive. They seek to keep people they care about in a state of constant attachment (sometimes even in bondage). In an atmosphere of constant criticism, they seek to control and direct the lives of others. Chicory types could be likened to stage-mothers, who place vicarious ambition for offspring above what love they have for their children. Toward self-seeking ends Chicory types can play upon the sympathy and sense of duty in others. When thwarted in their desires or designs, they are just as quick to play the martyr, perhaps evoking illness in order to bind others in sympathy or attentive servitude. They differ from the Centaury type for Centaury's martyrdom is borne stoically. The martyrdom of Chicory is intended for display; illness is selected for its dramatic impact. Not surprisingly, it is the Centaury type who often falls prey to the Chicory's methods of domination. Chicory also appeals to the Rock Rose type for their fear of abandonment and isolation leaves them utterly dependent. The Cerato type (who may be floundering without direction) or the Scleranthus type (who is in the throes of great uncertainty) are other targets for the Chicory type. The Chicory type appears to care for other people's happiness and welfare, but in truth Chicory is only thinking and acting from a selfish vantage point. They are like harpies—they can also be the Shylocks who fully intend to collect what they feel is due them.

Behind the grasping nature of the Chicory types is a need to be understood. They really fear dependence, which is why they seek the upper hand with other people. While Agrimony types yearn for companionship, Chicory types will seek companionship because they fear obscurity. They harbor a strong desire to be thought significant, so they enjoy company that supports that need.

The constructive Chicory types are selfless when involved in a "cause." They are leaders by example, never asking another to do what they themselves would not. They can be unceasing in efforts on behalf of others to "make things right." In this role they become like Spartacus—defending the weak and oppressed. Courageously, they turn their love of a good fight toward worthy causes. Their ability to probe weaknesses in others makes them relentless enemies of evil. They protest against the wicked, and rise in loyal defense of the innocent.

Scorpio
Fixed—Water
October 21-November 21

A study of this sign will offer valuable insight into the Chicory type. Scorpio is the eighth sign of the zodiac. By the ancient Hebrews it was personified as Dan, "a serpent by the way, a serpent in the path [zodiac] that biteth the horse's heels that the rider may fall backward."[8] This depicts a Scorpionic inclination to undermine the progress of the aspiring soul, coming at the heels of the sign Sagittarius. The rider is man's higher nature which Scorpio seeks to overturn by stirring his lower nature, the horse beneath him (the Centaur is half-horse beneath half-man). Here the serpent desires the fall of the soul just as it instrumented the fall of Adam in the Garden of Eden. This is a recurring theme in all astrological and religious lore: Scorpio as the pitfall of temptation in the soul's path and the serpent as the Tempter himself. Astrologically portrayed, mankind's "fall" (Libra, the Autumn Equinox[9]) is now what separates Scorpio (the creative act) from its pure or immaculate conception (Virgo the Virgin), and it is interesting to conjecture that these two signs may have been at one time joined—note the similarity of their glyphs—as Adam was so joined until Eve was separated from within him. This is heady symbology, concealing a great mystery that is persistent with this the most mysterious of zodiacal signs.

What is clear from these legends is how Scorpio is regarded as a stagnant force, seeking possession of the Power of Truth rather than allowing its passage. The Power of Truth would otherwise be transmitted freely upon the rays of the Sun to all mankind. Scorpio is the Lucifer of Milton's *Paradise Lost* who boasts "tis better to reign in hell than to serve in heaven." How else are we to account for the malefic reputation of this provocative sign? Even its ruling planets are counted among the more difficult ones to handle as far as astrologers are concerned. Mars is known as the regent of war, and Pluto as the land of the dead or its caretaker. Scorpio also presents the mythology of jealous defiance toward diety as well as a history of tempting man. It was the Scorpion that caused the horses of the Sun-chariot to bolt when they were foolishly driven one day by the boy Phaeton. (This defines yet another role for Scorpio as a "fool-killer," waiting to pounce upon the uninitiated who dares to assume a position for which he is not truly qualified; just as in the garb of Death he usually catches us unprepared. As this may invite lengthy digression about Scorpio as the sign of retribution, I shall only mention the topic.) Such a mean-spirited act had the dire

---

[8]*Genesis*, 49:17, from the Revised Standard Version of the Bible.
[9]See page 27 for the discussion of Libra.

consequences that it scorched all of northern Africa, making it a vast desert—so the tale continues—demonstrating Scorpio's inborn antagonism to authority (it is in square aspect to Leo) even to include its Creator, so symbolized by Leo's ruler, the Sun. Like Judas of the *New Testament*, Scorpio is willing to betray the Son (Sun) of God for a mere thirty pieces of silver, as such to reign for the thirty days of one lunar month (silver is the metal of the Moon).

Scorpio is a fixed water sign and suggests not only stagnant swamps and ponds, but also ice, which, like the earthly scorpion, is diminished by the Sun and its heat, as the serpent cringes from the face of God. Yet if nothing is truly evil we must find our "sympathy for the devil" and seek to understand the Scorpio presence as vital and necessary to the universe.

What is not generally revealed in these stories is that Scorpio is truly the sign of redemption and salvation. It is the seat of transformation. Only after having been tested is our true nature revealed—to self as well as God. That explains why many believe that God commissioned Lucifer to be the adversary of humanity as He did in the *Book of Job*. The greatest sinners make the greatest saints, at least according to scripture. Just such a scenario is behind the legend of Faust. Written by the great German poet Goethe, Faust is the Scorpio ideal, who, surviving temptation (and despite having sold his soul to the devil) is in the end redeemed and transported up to heaven by an angelic choir. Lucifer himself was once an angel in heaven, the Bible says, and will be again someday.

Finally, what we have is an appreciation for Scorpio's task as The Eliminator. As Death, Scorpio eliminates the excess population of all species, harvesting that which has outlived its usefulness. Harsh sounding perhaps, but descriptive enough, as Scorpio rules the eliminative organs found in the human body.[10] Scorpio is vengeful, too, but not completely lawless. In the Hebrew *Qabalah*, Daath is described as the invisible Sephirah (aspect of God). It is not shown upon diagrams of the Tree of Life, but is understood to span the Abyss before the Supernal Triangle, across which all souls must travel to become one with the Godhead. Rather like the River

---

[10]Note that Scorpio rules elimination, and if we did not get rid of the waste in the body, it would soon kill us—we would literally choke and die in or of it.

Styx, across which the dead are granted passage to the Nether-world. Death in every understanding and use of the term is a necessary prerequisite to a richer existence. Upon death, the Veil of the Temple is rent, and the son of man, the inner man, is resurrected. With such a powerful force motivating the character, it is hardly surprising that Scorpio-born people are generally regarded with a mixture of awe and reservation. Naturally secretive, these individuals never reveal themselves and are therefore difficult to understand. Clearly distinctive in Scorpio personalities is a pene-trating power of discernment, coupled with implacable will. Once aroused, passion and stamina combine with these to create a relentless determination that is usually irresistible.

CLEMATIS
(Clematis vitalba)

Bach, himself, described these people as having a faraway look in their eyes—indifferent, drowsy, sensitive to sound, with a pale complexion that reveals a lack of vitality.

Living more in their own mind and dreams, people who require Clematis are indeed of an indifferent state of mind. Inattentive, preoccupied with their own thoughts, they may withdraw into a world of unreality and fantasy—much like a crab into its shell—when confronted with any prospect of unpleasantness or pain. They make little effort to extricate themselves from conditions of illness or unhappy circumstances. Sensitive, they prefer to with-draw. And while they may feel a great deal, they cannot seem to permit themselves to care—so much do they fear emotional vulnerability. They can become masters of passive resistance.

Clematis types prefer solitude. They conveniently displace matters from their memory—and themselves from reality—in order to ease the weight of present circumstances. They are more at home living in the past while longing for the future. They are, predictably, lacking ambition or direction. Bach noted that they need more than the usual amount of sleep. This is yet another behavioral device that they use to escape contemporary situations.

Constructive Clematis types are dedicated to many social activities, and demonstrate a lively interest in the world around them. Receptive and attentive, they can become extremely creative and versatile.

Charming, thoughtful, and non-combative, they become popular, too, because of an ability to anticipate the feelings of others. With a keen sense for what the public wants, they excel in many artistic and commercial endeavors. Industrious, humanitarian, and practical, Clematis types are often involved with contributions that are helpful and profitable to humanity. They are enterprising and industrious, able to express or dramatize their innermost feelings. They may even do so on behalf of others who are less expressive than they are. Memory becomes highly retentive, providing a sense of history and loyalty. These people are capable of great sincerity and deeply profound feelings and thoughts.

Cancer
Cardinal—Water
June 21–July 21

A study of this sign will offer additional and valuable insight into the Clematis type. Cancer is the fourth sign of the natural zodiac, and it is a cardinal water sign, a combination that makes for turbulent and ceaseless emotional activity akin to the restless sea, the tides of both appropriately enough influenced by the Moon, Cancer's governing body.

Cancer, the Crab, according to legend, was rewarded with a place in the heavens by the Mother-Diety, Hera, for its loyalty in assisting its friend the Hydra, when the latter was attacked by Hercules. Pride and a sense of faithfulness coupled with a desire to defend the helpless are sterling qualities of Cancer-born peoples. The crab, known to discard its first shell for a second, has endured as symbol of the process involving birth and rebirth. Cancer is, according to the ancient Egyptians, the celestial mansion of the soul whose longing is as a longing for home. Cancers are home-loving, and fond of family, whether the family be the one into which Cancer was born or the family Cancerians feel compelled to create. A powerful need for emotional security motivates Cancer types, and they will pursue security with great tenacity. Cancerians live in their feelings, sometimes to a point where their acute sensitivity to inner urgings excludes all else. Not surprisingly, Cancerians secretly fear "losing their grip." They are easily hurt and prone to self-pity.

The more evolved people influenced by the sign of Cancer eventually learn that the effects of past hurts can be dismissed when we decide to dismiss them. Nevertheless, it seems that many Cancerians choose to remain sentimental. They love intimacy, they are kind, highly imaginative, and the homes and hearts of Cancerians are safe havens for friends and family. Cancerians nurture and treasure all things dear to themselves, having an eye for potential that one would expect from those ruled by the mother sign of the zodiac.

GENTIAN
(Gentiana amarella)

The mood of the type requiring Gentian is generally negative. These people are frequently overcome by depression and melancholy, or they are easily discouraged. Stubborn and fixed in attitude, they are difficult to cure during illness due to a negative outlook on life. They imagine themselves to be heir or prey to any and every disease or ill, and are susceptible to the slightest negative suggestion regarding their state of health. They lack faith, and are often heard to remark upon difficulties or set backs in life as being "God's will." On the other hand, they remain skeptical of whatever good comes their way; trusting only in "bad luck," and doubting

good fortune. They look for excuses to quit or complain. Materi-
ally oriented, and literalist in their understanding, they may remain
unconscious or unaware of the unseen influences and causal forces
that direct and shape their very lives. They fail to grasp the
relationships in things, tending to move blindly throughout the
course of their days—that is, if they move at all—for they are of a
resistant temperament, allowing inertia to overcome them, becoming more and more immobile. Appearing lazy, they are probably afraid to try something new.

An unshakeable faith in the power and laws of nature makes
the constructive Gentian type a true rock of resolve and determination. They can be a great comfort to others by virtue of this faith, by
setting personal examples of endurance and spiritual strength.
Their sturdy attitude and steady efforts make them an everyday
inspiration to others.

Taurus
Fixed—Earth
April 21–May 21

A study of this sign will offer valuable insight into the Gentian type.
Taurus is fixed and earthy, which says a great deal about the
personality of this type, for there are none more obstinate than
those born under the influence of the Bull.

Lest the reader should imagine that this sign is as graceless as
its bovine symbol, remember that the ruling planet for Taurus is the
delicate and refined Venus (at least until astrology recognizes the
Earth herself as the true ruler of this sign). Venus imparts an
appreciation of form, and a love of physical beauty to the Taurean
personality. Form—matter—is the special province of Taurus; this
sign is the matrix, the architect, of the zodiac. The traits of those
born under Taurus reflect this energy in the personal characteristics
of practicality and material values. Slow, but sure, these individuals
are steadfast builders.

Security and value are central issues to a Taurean. These
needs cause them to be especially acquisitive and resistant to
change. While Taurean values are usually thought to involve
money, we must not forget that this is one of the religious signs.

Spiritual urgings are expressed as a pronounced or overly exaggerated set of values, involving rules of conduct and a deep sense of morality. It is interesting to consider that Taurus was the prevailing sign over the *Old Testament* of the Hebrew religion. This is especially true of the Torah (*The Pentateuch: The Five Books of Moses*, beginning with *Genesis*), exclusively regarded to this day as "The Law." The word Torah can be traced back to the name Taurus as its source.

IMPATIENS
(Impatiens glandulifera)

As the name of this flower remedy would suggest, people of this type suffer from conditions of impatience and irritability. Quick in thought and action, they can grasp new ideas faster than most, and soon become intolerant of people who fail to move as rapidly. They prefer to work alone, unhindered, and at their own pace. Nothing seems to happen fast enough for Impatiens types. They get angry when illness overtakes them, for example (and "overtake them" is the right phrase, for they are always on the go), resenting its intrusion and demanding quick cures. They refuse to heed even nature's commands that they slow down. Lacking in discipline and self-control, they may be accident prone. They invariably rush in where angels fear to tread.

Rarely subtle, the Impatiens type can be outright rude and ill-tempered. They constantly seek to hurry themselves and everyone around. They fear frustration, for frustration eventually exhausts Impatiens types. Fear of frustration may be at the root of a preference to work alone, which is probably for the best because they look to blame someone else when things don't go right. An exaggerated sense of independence often leaves them alone and lonely in other ways. They alienate people with their brusqueness, fault-finding, and unsympathetic nature. They are not leaders by design—such as the Vervain type seeks to be—but are more like pioneers.

The constructive Impatiens type is capable, decisive, and frequently brilliant. This type can become a leader by example; a prime mover who knows how to get things done. The constructive Impatiens type takes charge, and is not found blaming others for personal failures or mistakes. This type can remain self-assured and self-reliant when the high ideals of the type are activated.

Aries
Cardinal—Fire
March 21–April 21

A study of this sign will further elucidate the Impatiens type. If Taurus appears as an immovable object, then Aries is the irresistable force. The glyph of Aries portrays the seasonal event of Spring. While looking like two ascending ram's horns, it can also be interpreted as depicting the first spring fountain bursting from the earth—or even the first flower. Aries the Ram is the ascendant of the natural zodiac, appearing as the first sign. Its nature is cardinal fire, bespeaking tremendous energy, which its natives possess in abundance. This energy is often ill-spent and seldom enduring, but this is not a concern, for Aries' energy is that of impulse, and not to be sustained.

As the first sign of the zodiac, Aries is the most primitive. By another non-derogatory description, it is the sign of unknowing or ignorance. Not coincidentally do we celebrate All Fools Day on April 1st. Aries' point of evolution is at a level of personal egocentric recognition. There is a child-like feature of Aries, an innocence that is not necessarily synonymous with virtue, however. Aries can be a very naughty child. This petulant personality is illustrated in Greek epics as the god of war (Ares) know to the Romans as Mars and to astrologers as the ruler of the sign of the Ram. The keywords for this sign are, "I am." It would seem the Aries native cannot help himself, he must, he needs, to put himself first. Audacious and as impossible to direct as Taurus is to push, the Aries person is authentically courageous, as well as irrepressible. The type is usually without guile, preferring the direct approach—me Aries, you Jane. These are men and women of action; they get the job done. And, if you can keep up with an Aries, he or she will make a very good companion.

MIMULUS
(Mimulus guttatus)

The type requiring Mimulus suffers from fears of a known origin. Such fears are the nagging variety—creeping, lingering fears that feed on insecurities caused by past experience, gnawing at any ambitions for personal improvement. The fears usually concern worldly events or material matters, for in these activities the Mimulus type seeks personal security and status.

The Mimulus types can be a wary and withdrawn group of people, yet they dislike being alone because they equate the condition with being ignored. They cannot accept the thought of remaining unrecognized, but a delicate self-image makes them unsure in the company of others, particularly other people in a higher social bracket. Mimulus questions personal weaknesses, disliking the thought of revealing themselves in any way. Feelings of inferiority drive them to achievement. Fear both prods and paralyzes them—fear of loss—fear of poverty—fear of being unappreciated.

People of the Mimulus type lack warmth and humor. They take themselves—and life—too seriously. They want to be respected, or thought of as profound and exceptional. When thwarted, they can become unscrupulous—simply out of fear—whether the fear is real or imagined. They long to possess the spontaneous self-confidence of the Impatiens type, or the poise of the Water Violet type. The Mimulus type often procrastinates, not because of indecisiveness as with the Scleranthus type, but because of a fear of the outcome of everything attempted. The Mimulus type knows what he wants and he lives in constant dread of not getting it. Unlike the Gentian type, Mimulus refuses to quit.

Constructive Mimulus types face trails and challenges, climbing "mountains" with a calm and dignified demeanor. They are determined achievers, capable of long sustained enterprise. They have learned through experience that justice exists everywhere and for everyone. They know that we all get exactly what we deserve. They have great integrity and fear for nothing. They trust implicitly in the great law of compensation that is cause and effect.

Capricorn
Cardinal—Earth
December 21–January 21

Capricorn is the tenth sign of the natural zodiac. It is ruled by the planet Saturn, which contributes to the Capricorn reputation of being cold, calculating, or mean-spirited. The sign symbolizes a personality that is serious, reserved, and sober, but this should not imply a total lack of humor. Capricorn tends more to the satirical, having a wry insight into life.

The symbol for Capricorn is the Goat, often depicted as a sea-goat. We conclude that this mixed emblem is meant to hint at the Capricorn's equal adaptability to land or sea, *i.e.*, that they are resourceful folk who know how to survive. A more delicate symbol for Capricorn is the unicorn, defining the highest achievements and evolution of this influence. People of this sign typify the sure-footed mountain goat that steadily makes its way over all obstacles, moving ever onward to the heights. In short, Capricorns are ambitious. They are also disciplined and reliable, and while they never take the risks an Aries might accept, they are persistently assertive in their actions. Capricorn is a cardinal earth sign, after all, so these people pursue material success with a determined resolve they seldom demonstrate for any other interest. They enjoy strategy, and desire executive command. This attitude is likely to foster some rather selfish characters. Ebenezer Scrooge in Charles Dickens' *A Christmas Carol* is probably the best example of the Capricorn's grasping ambition, albeit a fictional and therefore exaggerated one. Grown rigid and mean, miserly and pessimistic,

Scrooge shuts out all warmth and joy in his pursuit of money. The wintry affects of Capricorn have never been more clearly portrayed in a personality. Yet even Scrooge was transformed by the Christmas spirit—a reminder to every Capricorn that there is more to the notion of generosity than the exchange of goods. If Scrooge was a true Capricorn-type before Christmas Eve, we must remember to give the sign credit for his constructive behavior upon awakening the next morning, for Scrooge discovered, as Faust said, "Age does not make us childish, as folk say, it finds us genuine children even in our elder day." As in all Capricorns, there was a carefree, joyous nature in Scrooge—a nature awaiting liberation. It is no coincidence that the Christmas season visits Capricorn on December 25th, just as its spirit visited Scrooge. When spiritually inspired, Capricorns demonstrate a trustworthy and noble integrity that dignifies the personal life as well as the lives of people around them.

ROCK ROSE
(Helianthemum nummularium)

This remedy is generally prescribed in cases of emergency or great fear, and is a mainstay in Bach's famous five-flower combination called the *Rescue Remedy*. While the fear for which one prescribes Rock Rose is considered to be of the acute variety, there is, nonetheless, an accumulative affect and a marked susceptibility in certain persons to just such attacks. These people are represented by the Rock Rose type.

Rock Rose types are easy victims of terror. They are often targets for abuse, or are easily panicked. People of this type are veritable hotbeds for neurosis, being prone to diseases of the psyche. Unlike the fear of the Mimulus type, Rock Rose fears are the phantoms of the unknown. The fears are hidden in the subconscious, lurking in the psyche. Deep-seated terror causes psychological disturbances, metabolic dysfunctions, and glandular exhaustion, usually of the adrenals or thyroid. People who need Rock Rose are literally shell-shocked by what they have witnessed in life.

These people are pale of complexion—not from the languor that marks the Clematis type—but from a condition of fear. Their feet are usually cold, and the jaw is tight. Facial expression, although wide-eyed (even popeyed, as eye troubles plague this type, especially myopia), does not carry the look of wonderment, but is rather like a frozen mask of terror. The Rock Rose types often suffer from paranoia or neurosis. Nightmares threaten them or they may cough or gasp frequently, as if choking on unseen anxieties. Asthma sufferers are often helped by the Rock Rose remedy.

In this type we see a lack of self-reliance. These people lack energy and drive because they are already exhausted from the expenditure of controlling chronic, unrecognized fears. Left un-acknowledged, such fears will manifest in many ways (such as described above), in deep despairs, or tearful outbursts that occur for no apparent reason. Ironically, the need to be regarded as truly sensitive people seems to instigate conditions that in turn leave them vulnerable to either the vibrations of others or the environment. They become like emotional sponges. With Rock Rose types, fear becomes an entity in itself, and a fear of fear is constructed. They dread, above all, the prospect of isolation, of being abandoned. They carry a sense of loss about them, often acting as if marooned on Earth. This may account for their vague approach to all matters worldly or material.

Constructive Rock Rose people are true empaths. They are selfless, willing to sacrifice for others, loving because it is the nature of Love to love. They do good for the sake of goodness. "Bread cast upon waters" is the philosophy of life. In the words of the poet, "Through the hands of such as these God speaks, and from behind their eyes he smiles upon the earth."[11] They remain unworldly, but in a knowing, truly spiritual way. They are among the most evolved of humanity.

---

[11]From *The Prophet* by Kahlil Gibran.

Pisces
Mutable—Water
February 21-March 21

A study of this sign will offer further insight into the Rock Rose type. Pisces is the twelfth and last sign of the natural zodiac, coming after Aquarius and before Aries. Perhaps (with the possible exception of Scorpio) there is no other astrological personality more difficult to understand than the Pisces. That seems to belong to its nature as a mutable water sign; Pisceans are always being accused of being chameleon-like in character, taking on whatever personality to which they were recently exposed. Like Reuben, another of Jacob's twelve sons, of whom it is said, ". . . art poured out like water [by Aquarius], grow thou not."[12] Pisces—the sign of dissipation—never seems to collect itself. The people under its influence usually lack willpower and ambition, to a point where personal identity becomes of little importance. Perhaps this happens because Pisceans seek identity with something greater than themselves. This is (along with Taurus, Virgo, and Sagittarius) one of the signs of religion, and Pisces expresses through deep devotion and self-sacrifice. As the sign of Faith, declared by its key-words, "I believe," the Pisces symbol (the Fishes) was adopted by Christianity.

Jacob also said of Reuben, "Thou art my strength, and the beginning of my sorrow," and this describes the Pisces dilemma perfectly: two fishes swimming in opposite directions. A choice has to be made between higher aspirations and sensualist desires, to which the average Piscean responds with confusion. Pisces has within itself the greatest strength of compassion; sensitive to all things, not just to the familiar, as is the Cancer-type. This unselfishness is so pronounced that it often perplexes: one begins to suspect that it is motivated firstly because Pisceans never seem to know what they want. It becomes plain that these people need to express their sensitivity, even if it hurts.

Of their sensual side, let it be said that no sign of the zodiac can be more dissolute than a Pisces on the backslide. Their lack of resolve can be such that they fall prey to any number of harmful

---

[12]*Genesis*, 49:4, from the Douay Version of the Bible.

personal habits, slipping quickly into vague, sloppy and careless behavior.

For the Pisces, then, there is always a choice: between romantic lover or Lothario, devout mystic or idle hallucinator, to swim upstream, or to be swept away with the tide. Hamlet said it best for all his fellow Pisceans, "To be, or not to be: that is the question."

SCLERANTHUS
(Scleranthus annuus)

The type requiring Scleranthus suffers from indecision. Hesitant and uncertain, they easily become imbalanced and confused. They just can't make up their minds. In personal behavior they "see-saw" between extremes of mind and mood, and being not particularly sturdy folk, they are susceptible to having nervous breakdowns. Often they suffer from motion sickness or vertigo. Quiet and peaceful by nature, they do not seek advice in their indecision like a Cerato type would. Nor are they as readily confused by a myriad of possiblities. Indecision evidences when they are presented only two alternatives. Unable to choose, they will eventually reach some decision based upon their own counsel. It will probably take some time; thus they are prone to procrastination, not out of fear of the consequences (like the Mimulus type), but from indecision.

Lacking concentration, they appear also to lack conviction, appearing "wishy-washy." This occurs either because they genuinely see both sides of an issue, and are concerned with being fair; or they want to remain popular, a strong need in the Scleranthus type.

Constructive Scleranthus types are calm and assured regarding decisions. They trust themselves to know when—and if at all— any decision is truly called for. Discriminating, poised, temperate, they reflect outwardly the harmony they experience within. Fair and just, like Solomon, these people are sought and respected for their counsel. Constructive Scleranthus types are those who have found the Tao.

Libra
Cardinal—Air
September 21–October 21

A study of this sign will further elucidate the Scleranthus type. Libra is the seventh sign of the natural zodiac and opposite Aries. It is the half-way point around the zodiacal wheel, which is the symbolic astrological path each soul must travel. Its beginning marks fall or the Autumn Equinox. As has been remarked in the section describing Chicory/Scorpio (see page 13), fall or the Autumn Equinox also marks the fall of Adam in the Garden. Considered in this context, Libra is understood as the point of no return, upon which humanity remains poised in the evolutionary path leading to Aquarius. Often vacillating between personal progression and regression,[13] here at the half-way point human beings are equidistant from their origins and eventual goals. The sign of Libra being furthest from these two points, they have fallen into a state of ignorance regarding the true nature of either. As a result Librans tend to feel hopelessly removed from both the creator and personal destiny. The choice to continue onward is further complicated by the presence of the Scorpion (the eighth and next sign), which blocks the path by its fearsome presence and chokes Libran aspirations with fear. Little wonder that the symbol for this sign is the Scales, for at this point all things hang in the balance.

The problem of balance serves to identify the source of Libra's primary concern: to weigh alternatives, then correctly decide. "I balance" are the key-words for this sign, and for the Libra personality this means to do so in complete fairness. This is no easy task, and Libra is frequently haunted by the ghost of indecision, as has already been intimated when referring to the sign as the Scleranthus type. Still, Libra usually persists in courting this

---

[13]The words *progression* and *regression* are not used in the astrological sense of the definitions here, but refer to the progress of the soul's evolution.

challenge to a well-developed faculty of good judgment by seeking positions that demand its highest demonstration, such as that of a diplomat or magistrate. Librans have an innate sense of fair play and justice, matched by an exceptional intelligence about which they are especially proud. Those of this sign are often literate and knowledgeable for they love to read (we can detect the source of our word library easily enough) and write; Libra has produced a remarkable array of literary giants. As a cardinal air sign, its penetrating intellect is surely a match for its fellow air signs, Gemini and Aquarius. It follows that natives of this sign are equally eloquent.

Soft-spoken and amicable, Librans are intent upon being cooperative in social interactions. They love harmony on all levels (they love music as well), and sometimes it is an attitude of "peace at all costs" that makes them appear indecisive to others. This is the sign of marriage, and Librans' powerful impulse to wed is encouraged by their ruling planet, Venus, the goddess of love. Sharing comes naturally and as the opposite sign to Aries, the "I am" approach of Aries is reversed in Libra to express "we are." The glyph for Libra, generally represented as a modified version of the scales, can also be seen in this same relationship: as Aries is the rising sun (the ascendancy of the ego) the glyph for Libra can be perceived as a setting sun, attesting to Libra's willingness to set aside ego-drives in order to share.

The glyph for Libra can be viewed in yet another context—that of the highest justice to which the species is subject. This is, of course, God's justice, understood in our experience as karma. Science tends to define karma as cause and effect, and replaces ancient notions of a celestial or divine justice with modern impersonal laws of probability. While avoiding complex explanations of statistical principles, it is interesting to note the striking similarity between the Libra glyph and what is commonly known to statisticians as the normal curve of distribution. The symbols are identical, both in design and in significance. This curve, also known as the normal probability curve, is the scientist's explanation for the way most events are distributed in the world. This bell-like curve, as it is drawn upon a graph, describes the mean: the recurring and unerring result of what the scientist would ascribe to chance is what Libra reveals as nature's fair design, or an expression of a greater justice. When involving the affairs and actions of people this justice becomes "karma"—as ye sow, so shall ye reap. It all comes back to you in the end. In astrological terms, this is not difficult to appreciate when one considers that Saturn (the planet of karma) is exalted when placed in the sign of Libra.

By virtue of its position in the zodiac, Libra is the sign that best exemplifies paradox. Its glyph is also used as a mathematical symbol denoting "difference between." By incorporating Libran methods of comparison and moderation we are able to eventually gain true knowledge.

VERVAIN
(Verbena officinalis)

Of people who require Vervain, Bach had this to say: "They have the enthusiasm and excitement of the possession of great knowledge, and the burning desire to bring all to the same state, but their enthusiasm may hinder their cause. It [Vervain] is the remedy against over-effort. It teaches us that it is by *being* rather than by *doing* that great things are accomplished."[14] This type suffers from an exhauting overenthusism and the strain of over-effort. Champions of justice, they may become fanatical about their strong convictions—even power crazed. They are strong-willed people with fixed purposes and opinions. Possessed, too, of great courage in the face of danger or adversity. They pressure everyone around them with their special brand of fervor. They love to lead and direct, and often profess to being "chosen." The Vervain type is somewhat lacking in humility. They seek to transform the world around them (whereas Clematis types are more concerned with the world within themselves) and try to impress others with the significance and

---

[14]Philip M. Chancellor: *Handbook of the Bach Flower Remedies*, C. W. Daniel, Co., Ltd., Saffron Walden, England, and Keats Publishing, New Canaan, CT. 1971. p. 192.

sincerity of their beliefs and actions. Vervain types cannot bear the prospect of mediocrity, nor will they tolerate the affrontery of anyone who would question their ideas or motives. Thus they are easily drawn into argument. The Vervain types, being truly sincere, are usually completely unaware of how overbearing they can be.

Constructive Vervain people are proud rulers of their personal passions and inner domain. They grant others their due, and feel no loss of confidence or prestige in praising others. They respect the counsel of those more wise or more capable, for they truly know their own limitations. Cat-like they know, too, just how much force or energy is necessary to expend for any given purpose. Like the Sun, they are constant and inexhaustible, and may also grandly assume and fulfill a position of great significance.

Leo
Fixed—Fire
July 21-August 21

A study of this sign will offer valuable insight into the Vervain type. Consider the Sun as a descriptive ideal for constructive Vervain types. The Sun is the ruling planet of Leo, fifth sign of the zodiac. Also like the Sun, Leo has a fixed fire nature, thereby constant in spirit and aspirations. Under this influence one can expect that Leo possesses enormous pride. The Lion, symbol of Leo, personifies this trait. (We even call a tribe or family of lions a "pride.") Such a symbol also clues us to the great leadership capacities of those born under this sign.

A domain is essential to the happiness of any Leo. To rule over that which is exclusively their own is Leo's fondest wish. They seek the center of attention, and are at their best when being highly organizational—with themselves as the executive head, of course! Not surprisingly, they are family oriented, and family members are usually subjected to alternate dosages of Leo's magnanimous yet dictatorial nature. When not being regarded as little more than vassals, Leo's mate and children are very much the objects of Leonine pride and extravagant generosity. This is not entirely for show. Those Leos having a flair for showmanship and the theatrical make especially good actors—on any stage of life. The Leo nature is unswervingly faithful to loved ones. Leo governs the heart, and Leo affections are usually both constant and romantic, albeit excessively jealous. Negatively aspected, the Leo impulse is toward conceit and pretentiousness and they can be almost ridiculously pompous or affectatious, as well as being cruelly intolerant and dogmatic.

It is interesting to consider Leo in relation to its opposite sign— Aquarius. (See page 34.) These two signs are polarities of the same celestial force and are dramatically linked in the scheme of human evolution. These are the most blessed of Jacob, named as his sons, Judah (Leo) and Joseph (Aquarius) in the *Old Testament*. In eschatology Leo is the Son of God; Aquarius the Son of Man. It therefore follows that as the gods begat men, men shall become as gods. This is God's own promise implicit in the occult understanding of the Bible.[15]

As a tandem, then, these two signs—Leo and Aquarius— house the spirit, or what we know as the true ego in each man and woman, which presides over the earthly character and personality, and even over the soul. Leo and Aquarius are two of the fixed signs (the other two are Taurus and Scorpio) and all four are known in esoteric astrology as the serpent signs. This is due to the great, but secret, wisdom that they signify such as is represented in the structure of the Sphinx: the body of a bull (Taurus), the paws and tail of a lion (Leo), the wings of an eagle (Scorpio), and a human face (Aquarius). Such was the vision of the prophet Ezekiel.[16]

Not one of the more religious or devotional signs, per se, Leo's role in this fourfold celestial scheme is that of embodying the magnificent principle of Divine Authority. This symbolism manifests in society—or the body politic, as it is known—as both church and monarchial rule; the trappings of pomp and ceremony attendant to both being an expression of Leo influence. Even in the otherwise obscure glyph of this sign we detect this intent, for the symbol has appeared as the secret symbol of the ancient Egyptian priesthood.

Leos accordingly carry within them this legacy of privilege. They view themselves from the vantage of All-in-Self, while Aquarius, on the other hand, is the Self-in-All. The danger inherent in this

---

[15]See *Genesis*, 1:26-27; 6:2; also, *John*, 10:34; *Psalms*, 82:6; and *Deuteronomy*, 14:1. From the Revised Standard Version of the Bible.
[16]See *Ezekiel*, 1:10, from the Revised Standard Version of the Bible.

unconscious attitude is best expressed by the adage, "absolute power corrupts absolutely." The destructive power of the solar force unchecked is dramatized in the story of Phaeton and the Sun-chariot told to illustrate the nature of Scorpio (see page 13). Taken from the Leo perspective, it was the young Phaeton's overestimation of self that caused him to foolishly trifle with so great a power. Thus having made himself vulnerable to temptation (the Scorpion) he lost control, bringing no small disaster to the world. Such special endowments of skill and character as those granted as privilege to the Leo type must be exercised for the common good, or they will be overturned like the Sun-chariot. What has been granted by God to one servant will be denied by those who, in reality, are subjects only to God. To say this in yet another way: should the privileged few choose not to serve the many, the many shall serve the privileged few as a sacrifice to God. This present period in history may be one calling for greater flexibility and much adjustment on the part of all Leos, for we approach the Age of Aquarius, when divine privilege and recognition, once exclusive, is granted to all.

WATER VIOLET
(Hottonia palustris)

The types requiring Water Violet are of a profound and reserved nature which causes them to appear aloof. They are proud people who harbor feelings of superiority. Possessed of great poise, they can also be scornful or even condescending, acting in a disapproving, rather than autocratic, manner. They do not interfere in matters concerning other people; neither will they tolerate the interference or meddling of others into their own personal affairs. Live and let live is the Water Violet type's code. Keen observers of human nature and the human condition, they prefer to keep their distance. Thus they are never guilty of being tyrannical or domineering. Actually this type fears involvement, preferring the detached atmosphere that they have selected to be their own path in life. Although these are gentle people, they lack the personal touch of intimacy in action and conduct. They enjoy being alone because they feel self-contained and self-content. They love freedom as much as the Agrimony type, but Water Violet is more independent and highly individualistic.

The Water Violet type is multi-talented and creative. They are prone to suffering rigidities of both body and mind, rigidities that reflect inflexibility, strong will, and pride. Like the Vervain type, Water Violet feels "chosen" or select, but they are either too proud or too conceited to bother attempting to demonstrate the issue. The Water Violet type avoids arguments as being pointless and somehow beneath them. They feel no urge to explain or justify themselves, or to convince anyone of their personal views. In spite of this nonchalance, they secretly yearn to be recognized and regarded as unique and special individuals. They are basically self-reliant and self-assured, and do not have the underlying fear of frustration that frantically motivates the Impatiens type. The Water Violet type is quietly confident, and very patient. They will bear hurts and sorrows in silence due to a proud and aloof nature. This aloofness may be responsible for their withdrawal from their fellow human beings, at the cost of wasting considerable talent. When this happens these individuals wither and spend a great deal of their life in bitter solitude.

Superior skills and intelligence mark constructive Water Violet folk. They are altruistic and capable of great service to humanity. In this service, they are more likely to be found working quietly and unassumingly, without fanfare or display, from purely philanthropic motives. They respect the integrity of the individual above all else, and feel genuinely that each and every person has the right to evolve at his or her own pace, to seek his or her own path. They may become living examples of self-realization using the philosophy of love and non-attachment—akin to the "sublime indifference" of the Hindu or Buddhist. "The man of spirit is neither very intimate with anyone, nor very aloof" are the words from the Chinese philosopher, Chuang Tzu, and these words portray the constructive Water Violet outlook. They have dignity, poise, and a tranquility that exudes magnetic calm and soothing influence upon everyone around.

Aquarius
Fixed—Air
January 21-February 21

A study of this sign will offer valuable insight into the Water Violet type. The sign of Aquarius offers more varied expressions of humanity than any other, and is probably the most diverse and versatile.

The traits of the Water Violet type are certainly shared by this sign. Aquarians are very independent and altruistic, as well as remarkably inventive and original. To be sure, they take especial pride in their own personal brand of uniqueness. Pride in general is well-developed, yet seldom takes the form of snobbery as may happen with the Leo type. (But neither is the Aquarian as warm and demonstrative in affections as is the Leo.) Aquarius also shares the gift of leadership with its opposite sign. The quality differs, in that Leo loves to lead by design; Aquarius is seldom confident or single-minded enough for this. More importantly they are more diverse than Leo and prefer to lead by example.

The Aquarian reputation is based as much upon its brilliant intelligence as upon its role as the "true humanitarian." Aquarian keywords are, "I know," and usually they do! This is the sign for genius, just as its ruling planet, Uranus, is the planet of genius. The sign is fixed air by nature, suggesting great powers of concentration. The uncanny intuition of Uranian influence added to the Aquarian intellect places this sign a cut above the other air signs (Gemini and Libra). Fixed air also suggests that the Aquarian realm is the sky itself. Indeed, the name of its ruler, Uranus, is actually used as a synonym for the word heaven.

It is precisely this special intelligence that marks Aquarius as the regent of the future. Aquarians are said to live in the future while mere mortals must be content with the past and present. In the upcoming age named for this sign we are promised that humanity will fulfill its highest ideals and expectations. We discussed (see Leo/Vervain, page 31) how Aquarius is the Son of Man; therefore we can expect this sign to produce the finest examples of humanity in the great age to soon appear. Uranus translated means "light of the ages," and the Aquarian is often depicted as a herald of things to come. One example would be John the Baptist, who introduced the unusual ritual of baptism by water, and doing so in the name of the Lord, spoke of the coming of the Messiah. It is interesting to compare John's role with the symbol for Aquarius—the Water Bearer. Water is another representation of knowledge, which Aquarius pours out freely to all mankind. This sign is one of the four serpent signs mentioned previously. The glyph for Aquarius depicts a greater possession of knowledge because both the sign of the serpent and the water element are represented by its two wavy lines. The Aquarian response to the power of knowledge is very different when compared to the Scorpio type, for Scorpio would use this power for truth to its own advantage. Unlike the other fixed signs, Aquarius is symbolized by twin serpents to attest to the superiority of its understanding and wisdom over the first three. The relationship of the Aquarian's role as benefactor for humanity regarding the dispensation of knowledge (water) is further attested by the Christ, who characterizes his apostles as "the salt of the earth," the attracting and carrying agents for the "waters of truth," which they are commissioned to spread throughout the world. (Common salt is a substance corresponding to Aquarius; Natrum Muriaticum is in the pharmacopoeia of homeopathically prepared tissue salts.) Aquarius, the sign of knowledge, precedes Pisces, the sign of true faith; for as the Gnostics taught, true belief must be based first upon a true knowledge.

Another Biblical reference to the Aquarian nature involves Jacob's beloved son, Joseph. Jealous because he was favored by their father, and jealous also of his prophetic dreams, Joseph's eleven brothers conspired to sell him into slavery. Joseph was the youngest child and easily tricked—so much did he love and trust his brethren—and it was only at the intervention of Reuben, the eldest (symbolizing the compassionate sign of Pisces) that Joseph's life was spared. He was sold to the Egyptians, but only after being stripped of his coat of many colors. This coat had been made for Joseph by his father, Jacob (the Sun), and it covered Joseph in the hues of the rainbow, as the sunlight diffused through the moisture adorns the Aquarian sky. (The rainbow is the sun's "gift" to the sky—Aquarius—for its generous and unselfish out-pouring of its waters.)

To the end, Joseph's love for his brethren endured. He chose to repay their treachery with kindness and protection when next they met. So is the love of the Son of Man for humanity, the

Scripture tells us. This story of Joseph can be read in *Genesis*. The image of the Son of Man is repeated in other allegories throughout both the Old and New Testament.

To continue with our story, Joseph becomes the ruler of Egypt on the strength of his prophetic powers. He is able to interpret the dreams of the Pharaoh as prophecies of seven feast years, then seven years of famine, thereby saving Egypt from starvation. Once again the powers of psychic intuition are mentioned as part of the Aquarian nature, providing still another interpretation of its glyph: two lightning bolts carrying information in a flash of intuition that could never be discerned by mere intellect or simple logic. Aquarians often "know" without knowing how they know.

All of the above is, of course, only the "good news" as they say. Many Aquarians display less than these largely archetypal qualities. They can be unpredictable and eccentric to the extreme of being bizarre. In addition to being outright rebellious, Aquarius can be destructive in devastating fashion. Radioactivity and nuclear energy are governed by the Aquarian ruler, Uranus. Unrestrained, the Uranian Aquarian becomes a violent force—similar to the electrical storms associated with this sign. Uranus is the planet of cataclysm. Also of lawlessness, such as personified by the atypical Aquarian, Genghis Khan. This invites us to conclude that the co-ruler of Aquarius, Saturn (recognized as the sole ruler of Capricorn), is just the law-abiding, cautious and responsible agent necessary to keep the Aquarian's Uranian side from getting out of control. Saturn lends the serious, studious nature detectable in this sign, which often drives the Aquarian type to an extreme of melancholic solitude.

More constructively, the Saturnine disposition of Aquarius sustains that air of "sublime indifference" mentioned in relation to the Water Violet type. "The world is my country, and my religion is to do good," said by Aquarian Thomas Paine, aptly expresses the philosophy of this sign.

CHAPTER 2

ASTROLOGICAL INDICATORS
FOR PRESCRIBING THE
TWELVE HEALERS

We have now been introduced to the personality types explaining the twelve outstanding states of mind. Bach applied the remedies described to people fitting these conditions, and called them the Twelve Healers. The astrologer can easily attribute the astrological correspondences to each of the flower remedies. Bach's "state of mind" signatures, the corresponding level of consciousness or development represented by the signs of the zodiac, and the appropriate flower remedy for both can be found in Table 1 on page 40. Astrologers may find it more convenient to their symbolism to list the twelve correspondences in the astrological manner, as shown in Table 2 on page 41.

Some astrologers may want to consider the remedies in terms of polarities, as this is a common astrological mind-set. The polarities are as follows:

Aries/Impatiens . . . . Libra/Scleranthus
Taurus/Gentian . . . . Scorpio/Chicory
Gemini/Cerato . . . . Sagittarius/Agrimony
Cancer/Clematis . . . . Capricorn/Mimulus
Leo/Vervain . . . . Aquarius/Water Violet
Virgo/Centaury . . . . Pisces/Rock Rose

The polarity arrangement serves to introduce the twelve healers into the astrological symbolism of the polarity between opposites. You may want to consider the healers in their astrological triplicity and quadruplicity as well.

DETERMINING
THE MAINTENANCE REMEDY

The Bach Flower Remedies are used to heal by directing the essence of the remedy to the character, personality or mind of the patient. By combining the twelve healers with astrology, we can determine an astrological Bach Maintenance Remedy, which will work in a similar fashion to Bach's famous Rescue Remedy. For readers who are unfamiliar with this combination remedy, it consists of five essences: Cherry Plum, Clematis, Impatiens, Rock Rose and Star of Bethlehem. Only three of the essences used in the Rescue Remedy are from Bach's twelve healers. The Rescue Remedy was designed as an all-purpose composite for treating shock and emergency. It is widely used by followers of the Bach method, and many holistically oriented homes in both the U.S. and the UK wouldn't be without it.

The Maintenance Remedy, which would be derived astro-logically, is a personalized combination that can meet conditions of personality, character and mood that are diagnosed by looking at the natal (or birth) chart. This remedy is not considered an emergency remedy (like the Rescue Remedy) for its value would be in its long-term use. Using a Maintenance Remedy (hereinafter called the MR) would not preclude the implementation of other remedies when acute illness or transient moods suggest a need for them. The MR is an astrologically inspired complement to the individual for whom it has been prescribed. It is a personal antidote, but would be most properly regarded as a personal elixir.

The method for establishing your own personal MR is based on astrological techniques that only require the most basic knowledge of astrology. This information can be determined after the natal chart has been cast. You need to know your day, month and year of birth, as well as the time and place of birth. We need not take notice of the nature of the planets themselves—such as whether a planet is benefic or not—when diagnosing using this method. Only the signs of the planets are important here. The flower remedies are all-encompassing in their effect, having equal capacity to dispel or allay negative conditions while fostering and encouraging those that are constructive in nature. The MR will provide for, and protect against, harsh transits or stressful natal aspects involving the planets forming the basis of the remedy.

There are three simple steps taken to determine the MR. First look to see what sign the Sun, Moon, and Ascendant are in, next see what planets are located in the first house, and then check the sign placements for Mercury and Saturn. Let's discuss this in detail for a moment. The procedure is so simple, we need to be careful!

The most important factors in the natal chart are the positions of the Sun, Moon and Ascendant, as they influence the personality. Problems with the relationship between these three personality factors cause internal problems in the individual, as every astrologer knows. These positions are so important that the characteristics of the signs involving these placements will be an issue with the native. For example, a person born with an Aries Ascendant may have some of the problems associated with the Aries Sun. So the first thing you do is determine the signs involved with Sun, Moon and Ascendant. To consider a few examples: a person with a Capricorn Sun, Leo Moon, and Libra rising would need Mimulus for Capricorn, Vervain for Leo, and Scleranthus for Libra. If someone was born with Sun in Virgo, Moon in Virgo, and Taurus as the Ascendant, the flower essences needed would be Centaury for Virgo and Gentian for Taurus. We only use the Virgo essence once.

Next we look at the ruling planet of the Ascendant. The ruling planet is determined by the planet that rules the sign. Mars rules Aries, Venus rules Taurus, Mercury rules Gemini, and so forth. (See Table 3 for a complete list.) You need to know the sign the planet that rules the Ascendant is in. For example, if Venus is the ruler of a Taurus Ascendant, and Venus is in Virgo, the remedy needed would be Centaury—for Virgo. After determining the ruler of the Ascendant and its sign placement, next look to see if there are any planets in the first house that are not in the same sign as the Ascendant. If such a planet is found, add that remedy to your list. To go back to our previous example, if Taurus is the sign on the Ascendant, Gemini may rule some part of the first (or Ascendant's) house. Should a planet in Gemini also be in the first house, you would want to include that remedy. For example, with a Taurus Ascendant, the planet Mars may be in the first house in the sign of Gemini. You would include the remedy for Gemini in this case.

Finally, look to see the placement of Mercury and Saturn. Mercury indicates your pattern of thought, an important factor in the mental state for which Bach Remedies might be used. Saturn indicates a tender or sensitive area in the horoscope, and is traditionally interpreted as symbolizing a fear or a lack of some sort. Saturn can also indicate natural weaknesses that relate to health, so using the Bach Remedies to help the natal Saturn position may alleviate some problems. For these reasons, it is important to note the signs of Mercury and Saturn.

The purpose of making a list of the above mentioned planets is so you can assemble the corresponding Bach Flower Remedies, taken from the list of the twelve healers. You can then combine a special remedy, prepared specifically for the personality of the chart you are examining. Despite the fact that there are seven different indicators for the various remedies, you will find in practice that a frequent overlapping of indicators will occur. When this overlapping

Table 1. States of mind related to Bach remedy and Sun sign*

STATE OF MIND	FLOWER REMEDY	ZODIAC SIGN
1. Fear	Mimulus	Capricorn
2. Terror	Rock Rose	Pisces
3. Mental torture or worry	Agrimony	Sagittarius
4. Indecision	Scleranthus	Libra
5. Indifference or boredom	Clematis	Cancer
6. Doubt or discouragement	Gentian	Taurus
7. Over concern with others	Chicory	Scorpio
8. Weakness	Centaury	Virgo
9. Self-distrust	Cerato	Gemini
10. Impatience	Impatiens	Aries
11. Over-enthusiasm	Vervain	Leo
12. Pride or aloofness	Water Violet	Aquarius

*The numbers at the left relate to the Bach sequence.

Table 2. The twelve healers arranged by zodiac sign

ZODIAC NO.	ZODIAC SIGN	FLOWER REMEDY	STATE OF MIND
1.	Aries	Impatiens	Impatience
2.	Taurus	Gentian	Doubt or discouragement
3.	Gemini	Cerato	Self-distrust
4.	Cancer	Clematis	Indifference or boredom
5.	Leo	Vervain	Over-enthusiasm
6.	Virgo	Centaury	Weakness
7.	Libra	Scleranthus	Indecision
8.	Scorpio	Chicory	Over-concern with others
9.	Sagittarius	Agrimony	Mental torture or worry
10.	Capricorn	Mimulus	Fear
11.	Aquarius	Water Violet	Pride or aloofness
12.	Pisces	Rock Rose	Terror

of remedies takes place, obviously your specific combination remedy (the MR) will total less than seven different flower essences. For example, when the Sun and Mercury are in the same sign, two astrological indicators only need one remedy. If the Ascendant is in the sign of Cancer, the indicators would again be reduced by one, because the Moon rules the Ascendant, and you will have already determined the sign that the Moon is in for a remedy. To illustrate this further, consider the following examples:

Chart 1 on page 42 belongs to a person born with Sun in Pisces, Moon in Sagittarius, with a Cancer Ascendant, indicating a special relationship to and a requirement for the following remedies: Rock Rose, Agrimony and Clematis. (See Table 1 and Table 2). Because of the Cancer Ascendant, the Moon is the ruler of the Ascendant, and it is a dual indicator. We still have three remedies indicated so far. Jupiter is located in the first house in the sign of Leo—remember the Ascendant is Cancer—so this introduces

Chart 1. Sample chart for February 21, 1979, at 2:00 PM, Boston, MA. Placidus houses. Birth data is made up for the purposes of this discussion.

another remedy. Leo indicates the use of Vervain, so we add this flower remedy to our list.

   Look at the sign position for Mercury and Saturn. You'll see that Mercury is in Pisces, the same sign as the Sun. No additional remedy needed here. However, Saturn is in Virgo and signifies a need for Centaury. The total combination of remedies needed to make the MR for this person would be five.

   In Chart 2 we see the Sun in Cancer, Moon in Virgo, with a Leo Ascendant. We record only three remedies: Clematis,

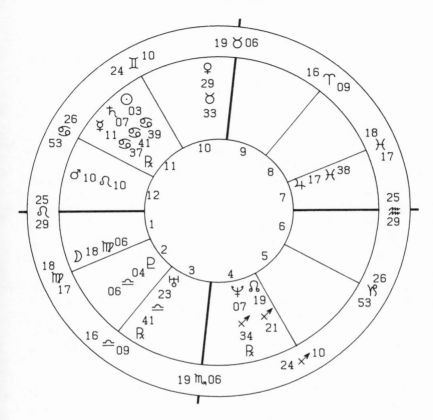

Chart 2. Sample chart for June 25, 1974, at 10:30 PM, Dayton, OH. Placidus houses. Birth data is made up for the purposes of this study.

Centaury, and Vervain, because two additional indicators are in the same sign. The Sun is the ruler of the sign Leo, so we will not add another flower remedy because of its placement. Saturn and Mercury also sit in the sign of Cancer, so we conclude that we need only three remedies—Clematis, Vervain, and Centaury—as the MR for this client.

Each person's chart is different, and you will discover that some people need one remedy while others may combine many. The average combination is four. Seldom will anyone require six or seven combinations—even allowing for the joint rulership of one sign. (For joint rulership information, see Table 3.)

The total number of essences in our combination becomes important for several reasons. The Bach Centre in England (where all thirty-eight Bach Remedies are prepared) recommends no more than six as the maximum number of remedies to be included in any one preparation. There is, of course, no inherent danger in exceeding this total. Charts needing combinations of less than six essences allow the more astute astrologer the opportunity to "fine tune" the flower remedy reading by taking into account any additionally peculiar—albeit less relevant—factors in the natal chart, such as the sixth or twelfth house cusps, or a stellium of three or more planets which may otherwise not be considered in the basic seven-step method of diagnosis. It should be understood that such secondary astrological features would have a lesser influence than what is indicated from the basic method we have discussed previously.

If you decide to add remedies to the MR because of specific horoscopic indications, they would probably be best used for transiting or progressed situations. The basic MR is intended for use on chronic, recurring conditions of mood, and this would be specifically prepared for each individual. If you add an essence to the MR, remember that it should be withdrawn after a period of time, and you might be better off having the client take it as a separate item. Under no circumstances should you create an MR that doesn't include the seven basic steps and the signs involved.

Table 3. Zodiacal rulerships*

Sign	Planetary Ruler	Sign	Planetary Ruler
Aries	Mars	Libra	Venus
Taurus	Venus	Scorpio	Pluto/Mars
Gemini	Mercury	Sagittarius	Jupiter
Cancer	Moon	Capricorn	Saturn
Leo	Sun	Aquarius	Uranus/Saturn
Virgo	Mercury	Pisces	Neptune/Jupiter

*In the early days of astrology, there were only seven planets. Since new planets have been discovered, Pluto was given rulership of Scorpio, Uranus is the new ruler of Aquarius, and Neptune is the new ruler of Pisces. Both old and new rulers have been included on this list.

As you can see, determining an MR is such a simple process that only a most elementary knowledge of astrology is required to determine it. That is, I feel certain, how Bach—a healer in simplicity—would have wanted it to be. If this sounds too simple for astrologers having a penchant for complicated mathematics derived from computer programs, consider Dr. Bach's own words concerning his flower remedies. These words can be applied to the astrological diagnosis as well:

> Let not the simplicity of this method deter you from its use, for you will find the further your researches advance, the greater you will realize the simplicity of all Creation.[17]

PREPARATION OF
THE MAINTENANCE REMEDY

All Bach Remedies are available in what is called a "stock bottle." A number of sources of supply are listed on page 73, but also check your local health food store, or even your local drugstore! People living in remote areas may have to order supplies by mail, but those living in big cities should have no problem locating stock bottles for the Bach Flower Remedies. The most economical way to buy the remedies is in these stock bottles, and then prepare the MR yourself.

In order to prepare the remedy, you first must have a clean one ounce (or 30ml or 30cc) screwcap bottle, preferably with its own dropper. Fill it halfway with pure spring water. Don't use water with "bubbles" in it. Add two drops of the appropriate essence from the stock bottle to this dosage bottle. When you are using more than one remedy, as we are in the Maintenance Remedy, add two drops of each of the healers that you have determined necessary based on the chart. This combination should keep well for several months as long as the mixture is kept sealed and cool. Brown medicine bottles are best.

---

[17]Philip M. Chancellor: *Handbook of the Bach Flower Remedies*, C. W. Daniel, Co., Ltd., Saffron Walden, England, and Keats Publishing, New Canaan, CT, 1971.

Should you want to keep the preparation longer, you may need to add a preservative. Some alcohol can be used. Bach preferred using brandy, himself.

Now let's look at an example. Turn back to the discussion of Chart 1, on page 42. The client would need Rock Rose, Agrimony, and Clematis, Vervain and Centaury. Two drops of each essence would be taken from the various stock bottles you have ordered from your source. These drops are all added to your one ounce dosage bottle that is filled with spring water. Remember, it would be a good idea to fill the dosage bottle that holds the MR you are making to the halfway point, then add the drops necessary for each healer, then fill the rest of the bottle with water. Keep in mind that if you decide to use a preserver, you must leave room for it also. One measured teaspoon should be enough brandy or alcohol to preserve the MR.

If you want to take the easy way out, you can go to a pharmacy that supplies the Bach Remedies, and they will make up the MR for you. If you work out the remedies your client needs based on astrological symbolism, especially for a client who lives in England near the homeopathic and Bach oriented pharmacies, your client can ask for the combination necessary.

A Word of Caution

The Maintenance Remedy should not be regarded as a wonder cure-all for major medical problems. To consider the MR as a cure-all would be to ignore Bach's intentions for his flower remedies. What the MR *can* do, in a constructive sense, is change the patient's response to the energies of his or her natal chart, so that an emotional and spiritual healing can take place within. Astrologers and doctors cannot heal. Only the patient and God have dominion over this. The flower remedies cannot cure any more than drugs can—the flower remedies can assist the individual's own natural processes by which true healing occurs. Four drops from the MR dosage bottle taken under the tongue four times a day is the minimum application.

The subtle, unseen, influences of the Bach Remedies on the emotional body can be likened to the effects of color or music— even to love itself. The effects of color and music are not easily measured in the lab, but are best appreciated by personal experience. Despite the stirring of the soul that takes place when listening to the great masters, we cannot expect that an invalid will be catapulted from a wheelchair to the dance floor—say, for instance, should he hear the first four measures of Chopin's A-minor Waltz! Healing takes time.

There are parallels between the healers, astrology, color and music. In occult tradition, there are correspondences between the signs of the zodiac and visible colors. Evidently our spectrum shows seven colors that may be seen with ordinary "daylight" sight, with five additional colors discernable only to etheric vision. The same relationship existing with the zodiac also exists as the cosmic pattern for the twelve semitones in the earthly chromatic scale. Much of this information comes from the Pythagorean theory of the music of the spheres; it has been corroborated by those who possess clairaudient abilities. While the zodiac serves as the sounding board for the heavenly music played by the planets, the twelve healers express in earthly unison with their zodiacal counterparts in heaven. Celestial sounds are made visible—like musical notes written down on paper—written here on the earth as beautiful flowers. Bach truly believed that God's love for us is evidenced in all things beautiful, and by such things we are made and kept well.

CHAPTER 3
THE ASTRO-PSYCHOLOGY
OF EDWARD BACH'S
SEVEN PRIMARY DISEASES OF MAN

Medical Astrology is the art and science of determining the diseases
or illnesses to which an individual is predisposed using the natal
horoscope. The utilization of astrology as a diagnostic tool within
the practice of medicine goes back many thousands of years.
Occult scientists would say tens of thousands—all the way back to
Atlantis and Lemuria. Even conventional historians have recorded
how ancient civilizations and cultures (such as the Chaldean,
Hindu, Persian, Phoenician, Hebrew, and Egyptian, to name a few)
have understood the precise and intimate relationship between
each human being and the forces of the heavens. And how the stars
and planets converse, exchange, and interact—both physically and
psychologically—with every individual on this earth. At one time it
was necessary to know astrology in order to become a physician.

The personality profiles and psychological implications cor-
relating to each and every disease, which have only recently been
rediscovered by modern physicians and psychologists, are inherent
to astrology and all occult sciences, being known to astrologers,
metaphysicians, and spiritual healers for hundreds of centuries.
These occult arts and psychic sciences have always understood
the unique relationship that exists between each person and the
Universe. "As above, so below," is the Hermetic and astrological
axiom applied to this truth. It was also understood that any
violation or discord in the celestial harmony between people and *All
That Is*, which is our "heavenly parent" and home, will coalesce disease into disease.

Millennia before the term holistic medicine became popular, enlightened physicians applied the diagnostic understandings of astrology, the natural medicines of nature, the spiritual forces of metaphysics, and all priestly Mysteries to the healing of men and women, restoring the diseased and infirm to their sublime status as the offspring of the great Universe. Healing remains today as a regaining of equilibrium, or the making of At-one-ment with the Unity that is the inexhaustible source of health and happiness.

In such an environment, Edward Bach would no doubt have felt at home, in agreement with the occult practice and philosophy of treating the patient and not the disease. In *Heal Thyself*,[18] Bach expounds on the metaphysical philosophy that all disease is the result of one "primary error" and that is acting against Unity, or the error of self-love. Self-love (or selfishness) grows from an illusion that the individual is truly separate from the whole (which is Unity). This is the beginning of all our collective ills and is experienced as illness. By imagining ourselves to be autonomous and exempt from nature and the heavens, we deny ourselves access to the One True Power which is of the universe, choking the power lines leading directly to the sustaining Life Source. It is then that we begin to weaken and wilt, like a plant lacking sunshine, allowing for disease to take hold.

According to Bach, this egocentric self-love produces first discord and dis-eases within the being, culminating in the disease of the physical body. Bach proposed that the one great healing force is the Divine Law of Love.

This "primary error," this "one primary affliction, discomfort, or disease," which Bach describes, can manifest as seven types, activities or defects, becoming the root of all our infirmities. Those seven are: pride, cruelty, hate, self-love, ignorance, instability, and greed. Each one of these character defects offends the unity that is *All That Is*. Bach tells us, furthermore, how the continuation and persistence in these ways—especially after we have reached the level of development where *we know these activities to be wrong*—precipitates dis-ease in the causal understanding of the word, which later develops into disease or illness of the physical body.

---

[18]Bach: *Heal Thyself*, C. W. Daniel, Co., Ltd., Saffron Walden, England, 1931, and Keats Publishing, New Canaan, CT. See Chapter 3.

In *Heal Thyself* Bach wrote first about pride. This is the kind of pride which "cometh before the fall." Bach felt that pride was born of the over-estimation of self, and due "to lack of recognition of the smallness of the personality and its [pride's] utter dependence on the Soul."[19] By this he intended the word "personality" to represent that temporal-self, the "one-lifetime facade," that mask of self-construction which Freud termed the ego. When this appendage of the greater Self, in its lesser capacity as a kind of provincial governor, assumes too much for itself, it becomes overfull and ungrateful much like a spoiled child. Pride refuses to recognize "that the success in the world is not due to pride itself, but are blessings bestowed by the Divinity within." Pride can cause us to lose our sense of proportion, for we are only one infinitesimal speck (or cell) in the body of creation.

Bach concludes, "As Pride invariably refuses to bend with humility and resignation to the Will of the Great Creator, it commits actions contrary to that Will."[20] We can easily assume that all people are, to some degree and at some time, predisposed to the defect/dis-ease called pride.

Pride is tied to self-will. The willfulness of pride sows and reaps its own unique and bitter harvest of physical ills. Those who are self-righteous, arrogant, or mentally rigid are prone to rigidity and stiffness of the body. Bach understood the relationship between personality and body, and the symbolism of astrology adds its own testimony to this concept. Paralysis may be due to an over-crystallization of will. Astrologically or metaphysically, this type of disease is linked to the four fixed signs, or to afflictions in the horoscope involving the planet Uranus (will). Certain types of arthritis or rheumatism are also involved in the misuse of will, especially those occurring in the back, spine, or joints (symbolizing flexibility) such as the knees (humility). In cases of arthritis or rheumatism the planet Saturn is also implicated. Saturn can express itself as repressed antagonism, indicating an unwillingness to yield and flow with the rhythm of life. Along with these indicators, the Sun itself (symbol of pride and ego) must be involved by aspect

[19]Bach: *Heal Thyself*, C. W. Daniel, Co., Ltd., Saffron Walden, England, 1931, and Keats Publishing, New Canaan, CT. p. 15.
[20]Bach: *Heal Thyself*, C. W. Daniel, Co., Ltd., Saffron Walden, England, 1931, and Keats Publishing, New Canaan, CT. p. 15.

if the personality shows arrogant or conceited behavior. In the Bach system, certain people are more susceptible to the sins of pride than are others. Consider people needing Vervain, Chicory, Water Violet, and to lesser degree, those needing Impatiens and Mimulus. "When pride begins, love ceases," no matter what type you are.

Of cruelty, Bach wrote, "Cruelty is a denial of the unity of all and a failure to understand that any action adverse to another is in opposition to the whole, and hence an action against Unity."[21] How many times have we been admonished to do unto others as we would have them do unto us? To love thy neighbor as thyself? Bach understood what all great philosophers espouse, the brotherhood of man, the oneness of all life, the unity of creation and its Creator. Mars has been called the planet of cruelty and all forms of pain are related to some form of cruelty. Bach recognized that pain, true to all laws of karma and recompense, will come home to roost, and each person will learn through his or her own personal suffering why he or she should not inflict it upon another. Cruelty can be both physical and mental. Afflictions in a horoscope involving the planets Saturn and Mercury make for mind-tampering kinds of cruelty. Add to this an unconstructive influence from Mars and we find cruel thoughts or bitter and harsh words. When badly aspected, Mars shifts its attack from speech to action when the astrological afflictions arise from Saturn and/or Uranus. We are all capable of the cruelty that is dramatized by the Chicory and Impatiens types, whether the cruelty is done intentionally or just thoughtlessly.

Plutarch spoke of hate as one might speak of an infectious and communicable disease. Bach shares this assessment of hate as being a true disease, and wrote that hate—as the opposite of love— is the reverse of the law of creation. He said it is contrary to the divine scheme and a denial of the Creator. The penalties for hate are loneliness, a violent and uncontrollable temper, mental nerve storms and conditions of hysteria, according to Bach.[22] Astrologically, the mood of hatred is most often accompanied by the astrological afflictions of Saturn and/or Mars. Violent temper and rage enter in when Uranus is involved with these planets. Mercury

---

[21]Bach: *Heal Thyself*, C. W. Daniel, Co., Ltd., Saffron Walden, England, 1931, and Keats Publishing, New Canaan, CT. p. 15.
[22]Bach: *Heal Thyself*, C. W. Daniel, Co., Ltd., Saffron Walden, England, 1931, and Keats Publishing, New Canaan, CT. pp. 16-17.

can focus hate into conditions called "mental storms" by Bach. Symbolically, at least, hate would seem to combine the actions of fear (Saturn) and cruelty (Mars). Hatred isolates. In astrology the same aspects indicating repressed fear, resentment, and grasping selfishness are those features that predispose one to the disease called cancer. Perhaps hate is a personality key to this malignant and destructive illness.

Bach maintained that the diseases of introspection, such as neurosis and neurasthenia, are caused by self-love. To ills bred by self-concern and self-intoxication we may add that condition of obsession or psychic disturbance. Self-love offends the Unity when we have too long placed our personal interests ahead of the best interests of humanity. In short, we are indeed our brother's keeper, and we must share in the protection and care of those around us. Such errors of self-concern bring to mind the flower-remedy types, Clematis and Chicory, then Gentian and Rock Rose. Astrologically, the water signs (to which three of these types correspond) are most prone to introspection. (Taurus, the sign for Gentian, holds a special distinction regarding introspection—that of inertia.) The other two earth signs (Virgo and Capricorn) also figure in this type of malaise. The chief planetary significator of this condition would have to be the Moon, symbolizing our moods and emotions. When the Moon (governing our feelings and memories) is badly aspected, we are prone to gloomy and dreamy states of self-entanglement and introspection, especially when the Moon affliction involves Saturn, Pluto, or Neptune. Pluto and Neptune may contribute to illnesses of the psyche.

Ignorance, as Bach explains it, is the failure to learn. Ignorance relates to a refusal to observe truth as it occurs in and around us. Bach adds that ignorance, aside from bringing difficulties into the affairs of everyday life, often bears the consequences of impaired vision or hearing, such as short-sightedness or some other sensory impairment or deprivation. Once again, astrology recognizes the relationship between mind and body; for in and under the province of the planet Mercury comes both the acquisition of knowledge and rulership of the sensory equipment of the physical body. Afflictions to Mercury can cause learning difficulties, speech impediments, or total sensory deprivations, such as deafness. People resistant to the finer urgings of the mind and soul, who remain deaf to the callings of our evolution toward enlightenment, or who blindly disregard fellow creatures, may one day find their senses failing just as their spiritual senses atrophied and faded. We are reminded of the Gentian type (so slow to apprehend) and the Cerato type (who allow themselves to become filled with information while remaining empty of knowledge). Astrologically speaking, earth signs most often fall prey to material literal mindedness, and when Mercury is in Virgo or Taurus these people may become narrow-minded or so stubborn that growth is inhibited. Yet it remains within the capacity of the entire horoscope, and thus within our very soul, to covet and harken to the messages of truth. "He who has ears to hear, let him hear."

Bach said that "instability, indecision, and weakness of purpose result when the personality refuses to be ruled by the Higher Self, and leads us to betray others through our weakness. Such a condition would not be possible had we within us the knowledge of the Unconquerable Invincible Divinity which is in reality ourselves."[23] Astrologically, instability results in horoscopes where planetary positions predominate in the more subtle elements of fire, air, or water. Earth and fixed signs supply ballast to the horoscope. The absence of planets in either earth or fixed signs leaves the energies of the horoscope "ungrounded." Thus the tendency to instability is increased. We observe this phenomenon exemplified by the irritability and restlessness of the Impatiens or Agrimony types, the indecision and vacillation of Scleranthus or Cerato types, or by the weakness of purpose in Clematis types. There is more to this instability than simple laziness. Bach mentions the more serious consequences of betraying others because of our own weakness. This can be as dramatic as the treason ascribed to Judas, or an everyday matter such as letting others down by our lack of continuity. Mental instability can lead to the same effects in the movement and coordination of the body. Physical instabilities can range from carelessness and clumsiness to the dangerously accident prone. The planet Uranus is often indicated in such behavior, afflicted either to Mercury (the mental activity) or to Mars (the motor activity).

Bach's message here is clear: people cannot allow themselves to remain struggling stragglers. Each of us has our duty to perfect ourselves and evolve. In the words of Marcus Aurelius, "Stand erect, or be made erect!"

---

[23]Bach: *Heal Thyself*, C. W. Daniel, Co., Ltd., Saffron Walden, England, 1931, and Keats Publishing, New Canaan, CT. p. 16.

Finally there is greed. Bach called greed a denial of the freedom and individuality of every soul. Greed precedes a lust for power. Ignoring the rights of other people—to develop their own way, at their own pace, or according to the designs of their own souls—the greedy seek to usurp the role of Creator, enslaving others in their lust for power. One is immediately reminded of the type requiring Chicory, and while so reminded, of how the Chicory type contrasts to the Water Violet type. Astrologically, such urges for power would likely involve hard aspects between planets in Leo and Scorpio. Pluto would probably be involved with personal planets.

The physical retribution for greed, or the desire to dominate others, causes the greedy person to actually become a slave to his own desires and body. Such disease will ultimately curb the fulfillment of selfish ambitions. When Pluto is involved, addictions or other compulsive behavior is possible, and will eventually undermine self control. Ironically, a benefic planet may become implicated in the more avaricious aspects of greed: Jupiter. When Jupiter is afflicted, gluttony—a most peculiar shade of selfishness—overwhelms the appetite in such a passion for self-indulgence that it will leave the stomach, liver, intestines, the blood—and thus, the body—in an utterly dependent state of infirmity.

In all the physical evidences of these seven "real primary diseases of man," Bach reminds us that the illness we get is no accident, for it relates to the law of cause and effect. While Bach was speaking about disease from his perception, he also espoused a basic tenet of astrology. The correspondences involving personality and the diseases to which we may be predisposed are significant to the astrologer and spiritual healer because they, too, know the relationship between the body and disease. Bach states, for example, that the heart—the fountain of life and love as he puts it—is attacked, when the love side of the nature is not developed or has been wrongly used. His views correspond with both esoteric and medical astrology. Heart trouble is indeed linked to the unfulfilled drive for significance (executive's heart trouble is one example), and the feeling of being unloved is an underlying factor. Afflictions involving planets in Leo are one astrological indicator. Leo rules the heart, and is a sign that best symbolizes a drive for significance and the need to be adored. When Saturn (with its contracting and constricting nature) is posited in Leo, people may be lacking in either lovingness or the ability to accept love, or may need to develop a feeling of importance. Bach offers another example of this principle, claiming that the brain is the center of control, and when afflicted, indicates lack of control in the personality. Such a correspondence is easily understood by an astrologer, for impulsive and reckless behavior is attributed to Aries, the sign ruling the head. The sign of Aries corresponds to the profile of Bach's Impatiens type. Furthermore, an astrologer would consider the presence of Uranus in cases of erratic brain impulses leading to, or caused by, a lack of control in the personality, because Uranus governs the pituitary gland which is also located in the head.

Physical and emotional correspondences abound: the hips and thighs relate to understanding; the back symbolizes integrity; shoulders represent the capacity for responsibility; the knees indicate humility; and so on. The kidneys, reproductive organs, hair, tongue, teeth, and gall bladder, all signify some aspect of the personality and the dis-ease that affects it. Blood sugar imbalances (such as diabetes) are often the result of some bitterness related to the emotional or desire nature. Each and every part of the body, when afflicted by disease, will provide illuminating evidence of defects of personality that are manifesting on the physical level.

For all defects and disease there exists only one true and permanent antidote: the Divine Law of Love. This law is, according to Bach, the one great healing force. He will get no argument from the philosopher, poet, or sage. The writings of all ages proclaim the power and beauty of that force that we call love. The astrologer finds love symbolized in the planet Venus. It is both fitting and assuring that this planet is the brightest planet in our solar system, visible to us here on earth both day and night. Venus personifies the brilliant and everpresent nature of Divine Love. In the Hebrew Qabalah, Venus is the planet of the Sephirah Netzach (whose title is Victory). This occult symbol serves to remind us that Love conquers all. Love is the unifying force that dispels greed, for Venus is the planet of sharing. Love restores instability to a state of equilibrium, for Venus and its sign Libra impart balance and poise. Love dispels the darkness of ignorance, for Venus is the Morning Star, the light of Prometheus, and the planet of beauty. Love converts self-love to selfless love, for Venus represents the "we" principle and is exalted in the unselfish sign of Pisces. Love is the antidote for hate and fear, as Venus is the antidote for an afflicted Saturn. Love is the remedy for cruelty, as Venus is the balm and polarity for the aggressive Mars. Love "vaunteth not itself, is not puffed up," and has not pride in the "I am." Venus is at home in Libra, the sign of marriage, and ideal love is at home within the harmony of "we are."

With love we can correct the defects, that Bach called our "primary error," the self-ishness, the acting against Unity. Each of us will one day remember that the part cannot contain the whole. Life is only limited and circumscribed by our mistaken notions or feelings of separateness from the whole. We are all the sons and daughters of God; one in quality with our Creator who is the everlasting source of love and power in the universe. The *All That Is* provides us the power for life, and the love to share with both fellow creatures and humanity, in an understanding that "one man's loss is no man's gain."

CHAPTER 4

THE 38 FLOWER REMEDIES

Once you have learned to determine the Maintenance Remedy using the natal chart, you will probably become curious about the other twenty-six Bach Flower Remedies. Less astrological technique and more personal judgment is required to use them, as you will realize after reading the descriptions of the remedies that follow. If you decide to work with them in your astrological practice, you should read all the available books on the subject. See the bibliography for a complete list of related publications.

Bach organized his thirty-eight flower essences into seven general categories. (See Table 4 on page 60.) These categories were briefly mentioned in the introduction when discussing the numerical significance of his classifications. With the exception of Classification 6, notice that one of the twelve healers is located under each classification. You will also notice that the lists are uneven—meaning that there are many remedies listed under Classification 6 and few in Classification 4.

As you work with other remedies, you will discover that many of them are complementary to the twelve healers and the twelve astrological types.

Normally the necessary diagnosis for a prescription for the Bach Flower Remedies is based upon an interview with the client. (Although practitioners have been trained at the Bach Healing Centre in England, and allopathic physicians, osteopaths, herbalists, chiropractors, and spiritual healers are beginning to use the flower treatments in tandem with their own healing practices, there are no "professional flower physicians" as such.) Bach intended his system to be simple, designed for use by the layman. When you use this method, observation of the client becomes vital. Letters written by someone applying for advice have to be considered less reliable. That the astro-diagnostician can use standard interview techniques is sometimes helpful, but not really necessary. The standard method of prescribing by interview is only as reliable as the intuition and perception of the person conducting the interview. Not everyone is capable of guessing or appreciating another's mood. Not all people reveal themselves in an interview. Even for trained medical people, the diagnosis of physical discomfort proves difficult enough, let alone attempting to decipher the subtle shadows of mood! That astrology can assist the standard prescriber becomes obvious, but the astrologer should keep in mind that it is best to adhere to the information in the horoscope and use the seven-step method. The

Table 4. Bach's Classification of Essences†

Attitude	Remedy
1. For fear:	Aspen, Cherry Plum, Mimulus*, Red Chestnut, Rock Rose*
2. For uncertainty:	Cerato*, Gentian*, Gorse, Hornbeam, Scleranthus*, Wild Oat
3. For insufficient interest in present circumstances:	Chestnut Bud, Clematis*, Honeysuckle, Mustard, Olive, White Chestnut, Wild Rose
4. For loneliness:	Heather, Impatiens*, Water Violet*
5. For over-sensitivity to influences and ideals:	Agrimony*, Centaury*, Holly, Walnut
6. For despondency or despair:	Crab Apple, Elm, Larch, Oak, Pine, Star of Bethlehem, Sweet Chestnut, Willow
7. For over-concern for the welfare of others:	Beech, Chicory*, Rock Water, Vervain*, Vine

†This table is from information provided in Bach: The Twelve Healers.
*Indicates one of the twelve healers associated with an astrological sign.

chart and the astrological method will always provide clear indications. In more difficult cases, or where a confusing multiplicity of remedies seems to be called for, the seven-step astrological method will clarify the situation.

The astrological method distinguishes itself as a technique for self-diagnosis and for absent-diagnosis. In self-diagnosis, objectivity, for all reasons human, is most likely to suffer right along with the patient. Your condition, itself, may impair or obstruct your view and attempted effort to help yourself, especially when there are thirty-eight remedies to choose from. (Pity the poor Cerato and Scleranthus types!) In any case, few of us are honestly aware of our mental and emotional status at any given time. Use of the astrological method would have already provided for the proper Maintenance Remedy, and a familiarity with the horoscope will direct you to the correct remedy for acute or short-term problems. In absent diagnosis, astrology is clearly superior to an exchange of letters by mail.

Astro-diagnosis can be demonstrated to be extremely useful in cases involving children. Children do not often reveal themselves with as much clarity as you may want. While it may be true that "kids say the darndest things," they do not, in general, communicate well with adults. Astrology removes this roadblock.

Here too the horoscope is to be relied upon as it would be for any other astrological examination—whether it be health or career opportunities. One of the safer features (and I use the word knowing the reader has already recognized that the Bach Flower Remedies are completely safe) of the seven-step method is that when it is adopted and adhered to, no fluctuation in interpretation can take place, for the skill of the astrologer is only minimally important. When you add to this the fact that the Maintenance Remedy is unique to the person for whom it has been prepared, you can trust it to be both inclusive and comprehensive in its effects.

One other beauty that comes from the wedding of astrology to the Bach system is that together they provide for a greater capacity to perceive character and personality—one which is transcendent, and not otherwise obtainable even from years of training in observation and counseling. Astrology and the Bach Flower Remedies work in harmony, gently urging and inspiring the person toward self-awareness and self-realization. The following list provides an overview of all the Bach Remedies available, presented in the order that Bach numbered them.

#1 Agrimony: Its astrological relationship is to the sign Sagittarius. See page 5 for a description.

#2 Aspen: This remedy is given for unknown fears. These fears are of the mind, and involve the sense of foreboding. The patient feels chilled with panic or fears some doom or disaster. The feeling comes without reason, and no explanation is forthcoming from the patient. The remedy Aspen imparts faith, and is closely associated with one of the twelve healers, Rock Rose. Like the fear that torments the Rock Rose type, the fear treated by Aspen is of the spine-tingling variety, in contrast to worldly, known fears that plague the Mimulus type. Obviously, Aspen should be considered as supportive to the Rock Rose type, and in all applicable ways as similar and subsidiary to the Rock Rose remedy.

#3 Beech: This remedy is recommended for conditions of intolerance and fault-finding. It's for patients who are fussy and in the habit of passing judgment on others, who lack empathy, or are filled with criticism and dissatisfaction concerning everything and everyone around them. Beech will impart tolerance and leniency to these individuals, allowing them to better see the good in things. It takes away that edge of meanness. It is especially helpful to the Impatiens and Chicory types. It can also be used as a complementary remedy for the arrogance and haughtiness of the Vervain type.

#4 Centaury: Its astrological relationship is to the sign Virgo. See page 7 for a description.

#5 Cerato: Its astrological correspondence is to the sign Gemini. See page 9 for a description.

#6 Cherry Plum: This remedy is for desperation. It applies to the fear of losing control of one's mental processes. People for whom Cherry Plum is helpful may be at the brink of suicide, or they may have thoughts filled with persistent and compulsive rage to do something destructive. They fear that they are losing their mind. This remedy is good for treating an uncontrolled temper. It will be found to be of assistance to the Clematis type. It can be used in any case where, after long-suffering, a person is in fear of doing something desperate.

#7 Chestnut Bud: This remedy can be used for people who repeatedly fail to learn from experience, who make the same mistake over and over again. They are "born new every day." These people are too quick to dismiss the lessons of the past. Chestnut Bud will impart greater objectivity to the personality. It is especially complementary for Cerato types who are constantly seeking advice and information. Whether Cerato types take the advice or not, they usually fail to correlate their knowledge and thus never learn anything. Chestnut Bud is supplemental to Impatiens— for the Aries types who are often unobservant—or to Gentian, for Taurus types who are slow to grasp concepts and come to realizations.

#8 Chicory: Its astrological correspondence is to the sign Scorpio. See page 11 for description.

#9 Clematis: A mainstay in Bach's five-flower combination Rescue Remedy. Its astrological correspondence is to the sign Cancer. See page 15 for description.

#10 Crab Apple: This remedy is a cleanser. It is recommended for people in a condition of mortification, or in the state of mind of self-condemnation or disgust. Crab Apple cleanses the mind and body of that which fills it with repulsion. It is also good for people who are in a state of remorse over some personal act, habit, or physical condition of which they are ashamed. It is of assistance to the Scleranthus type, as they seek refinement and detest coarseness of any kind. Also helpful to the Water Violet types who are prone to self-involved efforts at personal excellence, and therefore can be very hard on themselves in seeking personal perfection. Crab Apple is the remedy for those found harboring grudges or who have a pet peeve that they cannot release.

#11 Elm: The remedy for a temporary feeling of inadequacy. This mood overtakes people who are doing some useful or good work, but at times they are overcome with the weight of its significance, or the responsiblities that it may include. Under this kind of pressure this type feels unable to cope with the tasks at hand. Elm can be prescribed for this temporary mood, for this mood is to be understood as only a brief faltering of confidence. It is only for people who are usually proud of their work, who feel very special in their chosen calling. Elm is also useful to the Mimulus and Water Violet types, for both types are harsh on themselves and seek perfection although in different manners or directions. Elm is not, however, a substitute for Gentian, because the Gentian type's doubt is clothed in a negativity that sees no point in trying.

#12 Gentian: Its astrological correspondence is to the sign Taurus. See page 17 for description.

#13 Gorse: This remedy is for a feeling of great hopelessness. Under the burden of some "incurable" or "hereditary" affliction, people requiring Gorse have given up the belief that any more can be done for them.

#14 Heather: This remedy is for people who are filled with self-centered concern. They are obsessed with their own problems and ailments, and are constantly talking about them with anyone who will listen. The Chicory type, who saps the vitality of others, benefits by the use of Heather. In general, Heather is the remedy for those who seek to dominate the company and conversation of others with talk about their own personal tales of woe, and who are—not surprisingly—very poor listeners.

#15 Holly: Bach said that when a client seems to need many remedies, or if someone does not respond to treatment, you should try Holly or Wild Oat (Remedy #36), and it will then become obvious which other Remedies may be required. If the patient is an active or intense type, give Holly. With people who are weak or despondent types, give Wild Oat. While the astrological method provides the prescriber with a diagnostic tool of far greater precision then was available when Bach offered his advice, his recommendations are nevertheless pertinent to our understanding of Holly. By adopting the seven-step method, we eliminate any hit-or-miss approach toward prescribing. Holly can be considered the remedy in all cases where hatred, jealousy, envy, or suspicion are present in the patient's mood.

#16 Honeysuckle: This is a remedy for nostalgia; for those who dwell on the events of the past by longing for a happier time gone by, or in regret of some loss. Honeysuckle bears a strong resemblance to Clematis, and is very helpful to those of that type who are especially pessimistic.

#17 Hornbeam: Hornbeam is reminiscent of the effects that are characteristic of other Remedies. One such comparison can be made to Elm, for example, as both Elm and Hornbeam are applicable to people suffering from mental fatigue or weariness, especially when they don't feel they can cope with the responsibility of their work. The difference being that Hornbeam is for people who do not possess the pride in their task, or who, in fact, dislike their work. We might generalize to say that Elm is for the professional or career person, while Hornbeam is the remedy for the "nine-to-fiver" who suffers the Monday blues.

#18 Impatiens: A mainstay in Bach's five-flower combination Rescue Remedy. Its astrological relationship is to the sign Aries. See page 19 for description.

#19 Larch: Another remedy for despondency or feelings of inferiority. It has no apparent characteristics that would make it unique in its suitability, yet we can assume that in horoscopes where Cerato or Gentian are indicated as appropriate—being for those types as well as for a lack of confidence or feelings of self-doubt—Larch could be helpful. Perhaps, too, where there is fear along with feelings of inferiority, Larch and Mimulus would work well together. Be that as it may, Larch is a good example of a certain over-lapping repetitiousness involving a few of the other twenty-six remedies in their functional and comparative relationship to the original twelve healers.

#20 Mimulus: Its astrological correspondence is to the sign Capricorn. See page 21 for description.

#21 Mustard: A remedy for those darker moods of unknown melancholy, the kind that descend as a deep gloom and for no apparent reason.

#22 Oak: Specified for people who, while suffering, continue to fight on bravely in the midst of great difficulties. To these sufferers, Oak will impart the qualities of sturdiness and strength with which the name Oak has been poetically linked. (See also Gentian.)

#23 Olive: A remedy for any exhaustion or fatigue that may overcome mind and body. (See also Elm and Hornbeam.)

#24 Pine: Pine is a very specific remedy for people suffering from feelings of guilt or self-reproach. These are people who blame themselves for the errors and failures of others, and who always feel they could have done better—even when they have met with success. When using Pine note that these people are not suffering from any despondency or feeling of inferiority, but are fully competent and confident. They are also very exacting in their striving for perfection. Think of the Water Violet type or Vervain type in making this distinction.

#25 Red Chestnut: This flower essence is used when the mood is of great anxiety regarding another, perhaps some calamity or mishap will occur to a loved one. Generally prescribed for "fearforness."

#26 Rock Rose: Another mainstay in Bach's Rescue Remedy. The astrological sign associated with Rock Rose is Pisces. See page 23 for description.

#27 Rock Water: For people who may martyr themselves in an effort to set an example that will appeal to others or cause others to follow in their footsteps. Specifically, this remedy applies to people with high ideals and expectations, who are Spartan in lifestyle, disciplined in habit so that nothing will interfere or distract them from work or objectives. Their martyrdom is not of the self-pitying type, nor is it meant to attract attention in any other way so to trap or involve others. (This is not the brand of negative martyrdom practiced by the Chicory type, for example; for with any type needing Rock Water we detect the quality of self-discipline. The Chicory type has none, is manipulative, and seeks to discipline others by such methods. The Chicory type is more apt to make an example of someone else rather than perfect his own performance.) Rock Water is suitable as a supportive remedy to the Water Violet types who feel a great responsibility to carry their own weight, to demonstrate the highest standard of human development. Such aspiring intentions usually cause personal strictness. People needing Rock Water are hard-drivers who will forego pleasure to ensure the accomplishment of their personal perfection. They take their goal seriously, and so suffer from associated rigidities and inflexibility. Their discipline becomes personal repression. Rock Water is that remedy designed to relieve this personality, be it in fact the Water Violet type for whom Rock Water has a strong affinity.

#28 Scleranthus: Its astrological correspondence is to the sign Libra. See page 26 for description.

#29 Star of Bethlehem: This remedy is designed to meet the conditions of shock resulting from a traumatic event, or from hearing bad news. Along with Rock Rose, Impatiens, Clematis, and Cherry Plum, Star of Bethlehem is found in the prepared combination known as the Rescue Remedy. It brings comfort to those who are badly in need of consolation.

#30 Sweet Chestnut: Another remedy for those in the throes of some great despair. Sweet Chestnut can be administered to cases of hopelessness when a patient feels he has "come to the end of his rope" and can endure no longer. (See also Gorse and Cherry Plum.)

#31 Vervain: Its astrological relationship is to the sign Leo. See page 29 for description.

#32 Vine: This remedy is for those who would be king. The essence treats conditions of ruthlessness and inflexibility that are present in the ambitious leader types. Vine is for people who, being highly capable, seek to direct others, but do so in a domineering fashion. It's for those people who feel they know better how to think, act, and live, and demand that everyone else pattern himself in precisely the same fashion. In this way they demand complete obedience to their will, and display many other of the symptoms associated with a craving for power. The association of Vine to these moods of the tyrant or dictator make it especially helpful to horoscopes evidencing a requirement for the remedies Impatiens, Vervain, and/or Chicory.

#33 Walnut: The remedy Walnut imparts constancy and protection from outside influences. It is the remedy for people who need to break from ties that bind, to put away things that inhibit and retard growth and development. It can be used for people at the threshold of some major decision. Bach described Walnut as the remedy for advancing stages, such as puberty, teething, or menopause. (See also Centaury.)

#34 Water Violet: Its astrological relationship is to the sign Aquarius. See page 32 for description.

#35 White Chestnut: When an individual is found to be intruded upon or beset by unwanted thoughts the remedy is White Chestnut. It is administerable to people who cannot turn off their internal dialogue, who are constantly wrestling and arguing with themselves mentally. This is not accompanied by any compulsion, or by any fear of doing something desperate (the remedy for that would be Cherry Plum). The condition is one of an over-running mind, both questing and questioning. White Chestnut is especially helpful to the air sign types: those requiring Cerato, Scleranthus, or Water Violet.

#36 Wild Oat: This is a very precise remedy for people who are experiencing dissatisfaction with not having found their true path or goal in life. (Wild Oat is, therefore, a good remedy for reckless behavior or adventure-seeking.) These people have the grand ambition to do something of importance, and usually have the skills to produce. The problem is that they don't know in which direction to go. Their many talents only seem to add to the confusion as to which path is best. Wild Oat can be a very valuable aid to Cerato or Scleranthus types who are experiencing uncertainty or indecision in this particular area of life. Also to Water Violet and Vervain types, who usually have so much to offer. (See also #15 Holly)

#37 Wild Rose: Wild Rose is administered when the mood is one of resignation and apathy. It is very similar in effect and application to Gorse, being also a remedy for people who will make no effort (especially to overcome illnesses), who are quick to surrender in an attitude of "what's the use?" Supplementally, Wild Rose can be considered of value to types requiring Clematis, Gentian, or Centaury—all of whom, in their differing ways, suffer from a kind of insensibility to circumstances.

#38 Willow: This is the remedy for people who have become embittered by having to endure what they see as the biased and cruel injustices of life. These people have been felled by "the slings and arrows of outrageous fortune," but worse, have failed to recognize how often they also shot themselves down. People who require Willow see life as simply "not fair." They are the sorest of losers, and will never accept that personal misfortunes might be the result of their own actions and attitudes. They resent the happiness and success of others, and have a very begrudging attitude. They also tend to be ungrateful. They grab at kindness and favors offered by others with an attitude of "its about time something went my way." Generally, they feel cheated. Willow can also be administered to people who feel abandoned by the gods or plagued by the Fates. They insist upon only the grandest destiny, and having failed to receive it, will accuse any and all of having stolen or sabotaged their birthright. Clearly, Willow is a remedy of the highest value and service to mankind.

BIBLIOGRAPHY

Anyone interested in working with the Bach Remedies should read the available books on the subject. Many of the Bach titles are available in the U.S. from Keats Publishing Company. For booklets not available from them, you may want to contact C. W. Daniel directly.

The Bach Remedy Newsletter, available from the Bach Centre. See address under sources.

The Bach Remedies Repertory, by F. J. Wheeler, C. W. Daniel, Co., Ltd., Saffron Walden, England, 1952. Staplebound pamphlet.

The Bach Remedies, Keats Publishing, New Canaan, CT. Includes the following pamphlets published by C. W. Daniel (UK): Bach: *The Twelve Healers and Other Remedies*; Bach: *Heal Thyself*; and Wheeler: *The Bach Remedies Repertory*.

Dictionary of the Bach Flower Remedies, by T. W. Hyne Jones, C. W. Daniel, Co., Ltd., Saffron Walden, England, 1976. Staplebound pamphlet.

A Guide to the Bach Flower Remedies by Julian Barnard, C. W. Daniel Co., Ltd., Saffron Walden, England, 1979. Staplebound pamphlet.

Heal Thyself, by Edward Bach., C. W. Daniel Co., Ltd., Saffron Walden, England, 1931.

The Medical Discoveries of Edward Bach Physician, by Nora Weeks, C. W. Daniel Co., Ltd., Saffron Walden, England, 1973; and Keats Publishing, New Canaan, CT.

Handbook of the Bach Flower Remedies, by Philip M. Chancellor, C. W. Daniel, Co., Ltd., Saffron Walden, England, 1971; and Keats Publishing, New Canaan, CT.

The Twelve Healers and Other Remedies by Edward Bach, C. W. Daniel, Co., Ltd., Saffron Walden, England. Staplebound pamphlet.

SOURCES FOR BACH REMEDIES

If you can't get the Bach Remedies in your local health food store, or your local alternative health-oriented pharmacy, you may wish to write directly to the following companies for a price list and order form.

The Edward Bach Centre
Mount Vernon
Sotwell, Wallingford
Oxon, OX10 0PZ, England

The Ellon Company
P. O. Box 320
Woodmere, NY 11598

Martin and Pleasance Wholesale
132 Dover St.
Richmond, Vic.
3121 Australia

Scheffer and Partner
Eppendorfer Landstr. 32
2000 Hamburg, 20, W. Germany

INDEX

Numbers in italics refer to pages where the complete definition of the flower remedy appears.

D

death, 13, 14
depression, 17, 65
despair, 67
desperation, 62
despondency, 65
discouragement, 3
dissatisfaction, 68
domineering, 67
doubt, 3
drugs, 5

E

Elm, 63, 65
envy, 64
exhaustion, 66
eye problems, 24, 53

F

Faust, 14
fear, 3, 21, 23, 24, 62
feels exploited, 7

G

gambling, 5
Gemini, 10
Gentian, 17, 22, 37, 53, 54, 63,
   65, 68
glandular disorders, 24
Gorse, 64, 68
greed, 55
guilt, 66

H

hate, 52, 64
healing process, 46
health, 2
hearing, 53
heart trouble, 55
Heather, 64
helplessness, 67
Holly, 64, 68
Honeysuckle, 64
hopelessness, 64
Hornbeam, 65

I

impatience, 3, 19
Impatiens, 9 19, 21, 33, 37, 38,
   52, 54, 56, 62, 63, 67
inadequacy, 63
indecision, 3, 26
indifference, 3, 15
irritability, 19
intolerance, 62

J

Jacob, 24, 31, 35
jealousy, 11, 64
John the Baptist, 34, 35
Joseph, 31, 35, 36
Judah, 31
Judas, 14, 54

K

karma, 52